Raised by the Church

Raised by the Church

Growing up in New York City's Catholic Orphanages

Edward Rohs and **Judith Estrine**

 Empire State Editions
An imprint of Fordham University Press
New York   2012

Fordham University Press has no responsibility for the persistence or accuracy of
URLs for external or third-party Internet websites referred to in this publication
and does not guarantee that any content on such websites is, or will remain, accurate or appropriate.

Fordham University Press also publishes its books in a variety of electronic formats.
Some content that appears in print may not be available in electronic books.

Library of Congress Cataloging-in-Publication Data

Rohs, Edward, 1946–
    Raised by the Church : growing up in New York City's Catholic orphanages /
Edward Rohs and Judith Estrine. — 1st ed.
        p. cm.
    Includes bibliographical references and index.
    ISBN 978-0-8232-4022-7 (cloth : alk. paper)
1. Rohs, Edward, 1946–   2. Orphans—New York (State)—New York—Biography.
3. Children—Institutional care—New York (State)—New York.   4. Orphanages—
New York (State)—New York.   5. Church work with orphans—Catholic Church.
I. Estrine, Judith.   II. Title.
    HV995.N49R64 2012
    362.73′2—dc23
    [B]

                                                                    2011026396

Printed in the United States of America
14 13 12   5 4 3 2 1
First edition

To Elsie Pascrell

Contents

My Ten Beliefs for Success

1. Always go after your dreams, even if they seem beyond your reach.
2. Always believe in yourself, even if you are the only one.
3. Always accept that obstacles and setbacks are inevitable in your pursuit of goals and dreams.
4. Always remember that determination and passion are key components for success.
5. Always surround yourself with people from whom you can learn.
6. Always try to be assertive and perform beyond what people expect or require of you.
7. Always aim high and keep raising the bar.
8. Always take responsibility for things that are under your control.
9. Always remember that loyalty is as important as competency.
10. Always go with your instincts and gut feelings when you are not sure what to do.

Acknowledgments

We are grateful for the contribution of many people to this book: Eric Newman, Fordham University Press's managing editor; Laura Wood, our agent at FinePrint; Peter Barksdale at the New York Public Library; and Nicholas Taylor, our copy editor. We thank Peter Vaughan and William Seraile for their careful reading of the manuscript and acknowledge the support of Geraldine Flaherty, Monsignor Robert M. Harris, Father Paul Landolfi, James McCann, Rita E. Moran, Father Joseph O'Hare, Tom Penders, Joseph Reilly, Robert Rohs, and Marilyn Sachar. Thanks also to Fred Nachbaur, Kate O'Brien-Nicholson and Kathleen A. Sweeney, and Tara Kennedy. And finally, our love and gratitude to Steven Estrine, without whom this book would never have happened.

Prologue

I was born on March 23, 1946, and abandoned six months later when my mother, Viola Best, brought me to the Angel Guardian Home to be raised by the Sisters of Mercy. A couple of months later she and my father, Edward Rohs, formalized the arrangement by signing papers that made the church temporarily responsible for my upbringing.

My parents may have believed that in time they would take me back, so they did not sign papers giving up their parental rights. Without their signatures on that document, I could never be legally adopted.

Eventually they married, and nine years after I was born my mother gave birth to twins, Robert and Barbara, whom she and my father raised in a housing project in Queens. But they never claimed me. And they never got around to signing those papers. Legally, I remained a ward of New York state.

I grew up under Catholic auspices in institutional homes, now known as congregate foster care, and resided in five agencies throughout my childhood. Principally acting *in loco parentis* and under authority entrusted to them by the governor of the state of New York, these agencies were responsible for my maintenance, growth, and development until I was legally emancipated at age eighteen.

Introduction

Hollywood loves its orphans. Any given year you are likely to find at least one movie involving a parentless child. The plot usually turns on one of the following scenarios:

Storyline #1. Orphan is feisty but also pathetically grateful to be given the chance to become part of a "normal" family in a "normal" environment. This orphan may be amusing or sad. He or she is adorable.

Storyline #2. Orphan is vengeful and so jealous of everyone that he or she repays benefactors by murdering them off, one at a time (vampire twist optional).

Storyline #3. Orphan languishes in a cold institution until a couple arrives unannounced. They are looking for their child, who, by some strange event, has been taken from them. They have one baby picture. If the movie is G-rated, they find the child and everyone lives happily ever after. If it is released to theaters on Halloween, the orphan is a homicidal stalker with a carving knife.

Storyline #3A. #3 as a musical. The wife is barren and the tyke cuter than cute. Lose the knife.

But there is another storyline, and it involves no knives and definitely no parents desperate to claim their son. But it is a true story, and it is mine. Before I was one year old and until I graduated from high school at nineteen, I was raised in five Catholic orphanages. I was not bounced from place to place because I was an unwanted problem child. I did not smash windows and I did not burn anything down. I was not a bad kid. Ask the nuns who raised me. They will tell you I was a good little boy with an impish grin and an overwhelming need to please.

I was moved around because the Catholic orphanage system in the 1950s and 1960s separated children by age and by gender. It was a silo system of childcare. Boys (and girls) within a particular age group stayed in an institution until they "aged out" and were sent on to the next "home." Under this system, every few years I was transferred to the next school level in a different institutional setting in a different neighborhood. I received a strict parochial education at each school. One day, without fanfare and with minimal warning, a black plastic garbage bag would appear on my bed. I would be ordered to fill it with my few necessities, and then, along with other boys assigned to the same new location, I was driven in our institution's vehicle from the place we had come to know as "home" to a new "home."

I spent two years at the Angel Guardian Home, but then they moved me to the Convent of Mercy Home. Five years later, I went to St. Mary of the Angel Home, followed by St. John's Home for Boys, and finally St. Vincent's Home for Boys. St. Vincent's was my last stop before I was discharged from the Catholic orphanage system into the real world.

Looking back on that time, I believe that the closest parallel to my experiences are those of "army brats"—the kids of career service members who move to new bases when they receive orders from their superior officers. Like them, I received my "marching orders" to pack up and move. Like army brats, I had to start from scratch, figuring out who the bullies were and where they hung out, and forming alliances so I could fit in. But the similarities end there.

On the plus side, my buddies usually came with me and we tried, as best we could, to protect one another. On the minus side, unlike

parents in these situations, my adult c
with me when I moved. There were n
for me when I got home from school
vided continuity in the frequently cha

When I moved to a new institutio
who were charged with my care. At
of Mercy in their convent orphanage
I was turned over to the Marianist I
well-meaning social worker clued me
to the Catholic orphanage system in tin ...
I was different from the other boys I saw in church or the kids who
came to pay a charitable visit with their parents at Christmas.

How come they have mothers and I have nuns?

Ah, those nuns—my caregivers and the keepers of my known
world—stern guardians of the straight and narrow. There was no
way a fellow could confuse them with Donna Reed. They knew who
I was and the secret of how I came to live in an institution instead of
in a normal house. It was a secret they never revealed.

I remember being lonely, but I was never alone—not ever. I lived
in dormitories with dozens of boys. They were the friends I grew up
with, the guys who shared the showers, the schedules, the institutional cooking. We went to the same Catholic school on the institution's grounds, where we were taught by mostly the same people
who woke us up in the morning and shot us dirty looks when we
giggled at Mass. (The only exceptions were a few teachers sent from
the board of education to handle subjects in the curriculum that the
school was not equipped to teach.)

The boys were less than siblings but much more than acquain-
tances. We were a cadre of vulnerable kids who had learned how to
survive in whatever environment we found ourselves. I lost contact
with many of them after we were finally dismissed from the system.
Some succumbed to a life of drugs and drug-related crimes but others made it out alive and intact, and we remain friends to this day
(see Appendix A).

After graduating from John Jay High School and leaving the Catholic orphanage system that had raised me, I made a conscious decision to keep quiet about my upbringing. I figured that if I told people, they would flee or at least feel very sorry for me—even sorrier than I felt for myself. I also made a conscious effort to change my destiny by emulating the men I had admired as a kid. I earned an advanced degree and expanded my world. I tried to learn from people who had earned positions of authority and respect, and I developed friendships with good men and women. I often got together with the boys—now men—who had made something of themselves after leaving the Catholic institution system. And I tried to fulfill my sense of obligation and passion for helping the next generation of homeless, abused, and abandoned boys—boys like me—by working on their behalf, first within the system I came from and then, for many years, with the New York State Office of Mental Health. I received numerous government awards and a presidential commendation acknowledging my work.

But I never spoke about my past to anyone. It was my secret—a shameful secret. They vaguely knew that I had a past that was different from theirs, but they were ignorant about the particulars.

Then, one lovely evening as I was being honored at an alumni award dinner at Fordham University, I had what can only be described as an epiphany. Maybe it was seeing tables of friends and colleagues, people I trusted, beaming at me as I stepped up to deliver my speech. Or maybe it was just time for me to get closure on my past and finally move on. It was time to acknowledge that even though I had been raised in an institution, this experience no longer defined me. It was time to share my story because, finally, there was no shame.

And as I spoke, I saw jaws drop and tears shed. My colleague and friend Steve Estrine was in the audience, and later, as we sat chatting, he urged me to bring my story to the public. I told him I had already written a first draft of a memoir. Later that night, he told my story to his wife, Judith, who is a writer. She called me to express her interest in reading my manuscript; after reading it, she agreed that it was a story worth telling. And so Judith and I—and Steve, when he could get away—began meeting on Wednesdays at four thirty to refine my original manuscript. We visited the Catholic institutions where I had lived, and we interviewed the sisters and brothers who had helped raise me. We pored over old magazines and newspapers and I dug up pictures and memorabilia. Mostly, though, I spoke and Judith listened. Somewhere in the process a history-minded friend pointed out that I was part of a bigger story, which began more than a century before I was born: Protestant, Jewish, and Catholic religious communities in the 1800s each worked to meet a huge need, struggling to care for millions of homeless, orphaned, and abandoned children, as well as the children of casualties of the Civil War and the conflicts that followed.

We found the idea tantalizing and at first thought to explore the various ethnic and religious groups who assumed the mantle of responsibility—a fascinating story. But in the end, we decided to limit our tale to the Catholic experience in the New York City area. This book gives a broad historic overview of how American society attempted to meet the needs of its vulnerable children, but its primary focus is on my experiences in institutional homes in Brooklyn, Queens, and Long Island. It is the true story of how I was raised by the church.

Orphans in America

God is the father of orphans.

Psalm 68:6

1   **The Search for Solutions**

It's a fantasy to imagine that our complex world has somehow lost its ability to provide compassionate care for the most vulnerable children in our society. It's a fantasy to believe that if we could only go back to the "good old days" the thorny issues would dis appear.

This book tells the story of how people of goodwill worked to find consensus among the conflicting philosophical, political, and moral beliefs about society's role in caring for the poor. It is a story of the constant debates about our obligations to the smallest and most vulnerable among us, because the truth is that there was never a golden time when conscientious people did not struggle with these issues.

Long before the American Revolution, colonists wrestled with the same questions that confound us today: How can society provide impoverished, orphaned and abandoned children with the tools to become contributing members of society? Where should they live? Who will care for them? How much will such care cost? And, of course, who will pay the bills?

In the 1960s, the federal government mandated that orphanages be closed. Foster care became "the answer," which is interesting because before foster care, orphanages were "the answer," filling the role of caregivers to young children. Before that, the solution was to indenture minors and ship thousands of urban children to rural settings in the Midwest on "orphan trains." And before orphanages and orphan trains, institutions known variously in this country as "the poorhouse," "the poor farm," or "the workhouse" provided children and their indigent parents with custodial care.

The Poorhouse

As early as 1653, the Dutch community of New Amsterdam—later New York City—appointed two men as "Overseers of Orphans." Their responsibilities were to "keep their eyes open and look . . . after widows and orphans." The Dutch also created an Orphan's Court to "attend to orphans and minor children within the jurisdiction of this city." These early institutions were the first acknowledgement by early settlers that, in the absence of parental supervision, the community had a moral responsibility to care for its young.

A few years later, Boston made an official commitment when, in 1660, it created the first legislated social safety net in colonial America—the poorhouse. City leaders were influenced by the English Poor Laws, which made the surrounding community responsible for keeping orphans and widows from dying of starvation. Boston's poorhouse was a pungent mix of humanity that included the aged, alcoholic, disabled, mentally ill, unemployed, widowed, and children. Before there was Social Security, unemployment insurance, Medicare, Medicaid, or food stamps, the poorhouse provided millions of Americans with its scant aid and comfort.

Still, limited as it was, the poorhouse met an urgent need. As settlers expanded west across North America, they were sure to build poorhouses in addition to churches and schools. In time, some of these humble institutions evolved into full-fledged community resources. In some counties and towns, while remaining available for its original use, the local poorhouse grew to play a major role as an agricultural center and was reinvented as a source of revenue for the government.

But a safety net can stretch only so far before it begins to tear. As the population grew, so, too, did the poorhouse population, and by the 1820s conditions there ranged from barely tolerable to horrific. Usually, the institution's administrator held his position only because of political patronage. It was an early example of a "no-show" job. The average administrator did as little as he could, which was in line with the thinking of the poorhouse governing body, whose aim was to spend as little money as was absolutely necessary. This neglect translated into the horror stories that have come down to us from that time: people with mental and emotional disabilities chained to the wall and treated like animals; criminals and alcoholics lurching in the halls, terrifying children and preying on old men and women; and the like.

The Deserving Versus the Undeserving Poor

By the 1840s, people could not pretend that the poorhouse was an acceptable answer; conditions there became so awful and the taint of criminal negligence so obvious that society could no longer get away with its benign neglect. Muckrakers like Dorothea Dix campaigned on behalf of the mentally ill, and the wealthy, educated classes in both the United States and Great Britain engaged in passionate debate. Should the "deserving poor"—that is, children, the mentally ill, and the aged—be treated the same as alcoholics and able-bodied vagrants (the "undeserving poor")? This led to another, stickier question: Was it right that the "deserving" children of "undeserving poor" parents be made to stay in the poorhouse with them, or should they be moved to a more rarified environment?

In *Pygmalion,* George Bernard Shaw satirizes society's tendency to neatly characterize impoverished people as either "deserving" or "undeserving" poor. Eliza Doolittle's roustabout, heavy-drinking father declines a generous handout, announcing that he is one of the "undeserving poor" and that he wants to keep it that way.

Nevertheless, a movement took shape, built on the premise that children living in poorhouses would be much better off if they were taken from their parents and installed in a more genteel environment. What could be wrong with moving young people away from the degenerative poorhouses? Who could object to bringing children into a protective environment, giving them every advantage and the opportunity to flourish? Men of goodwill imagined an ideal world, with routine, discipline, and regimentation converting all but the most hardened street urchin into model citizens.

The Orphanage Is "The Answer"

And so it happened that well-meaning philanthropists and religious societies established orphanages—society's newest solution to the perennial problem of what to do with parentless and abandoned children. For a short while, these institutions succeeded in realizing the utopian ideals of their founders. A few lucky children were nurtured and protected, and yes, they grew up to be law-abiding citizens. But of course the experiment failed. Setting aside the questionable ethics of snatching children away from their parents, there was the more practical problem of where to put them. The orphanage as originally designed was a contradiction: an elite institution that was free and open to all needy children.

Once again, the safety net could not hold. The number of children who needed to be taken in and cared for far outnumbered the available beds. And it certainly was too expensive for the governments paying the bills. It became impossible to build orphanages quickly enough. Reality overcame fantasy, and nowhere was "reality" harsher and more in evidence than in New York City, whose system, for better or worse, became the template for orphanages being built around the country. That is why the history of the orphanage in the United States begins there, and in its sister city across the water, Brooklyn.

2 New York City in the Nineteenth Century

Between 1810 and 1860, New York City's population grew from 119,734 to 1,174,799, in large part because of a huge influx of immigrants from Ireland, Wales, and Germany. Being a port of entry, New York was the place where most immigrants settled, and the majority of these immigrants were desperate for work. Some men left the immediate urban area and got jobs working on the Erie Canal, living on edge of subsistence—some for fifty cents a day and jiggers of whiskey. Like most immigrant groups coming to the United States, the Erie Canal workers labored at jobs nobody else wanted. It was backbreaking and dangerous and they died by the thousands, of malaria, yellow fever, and cholera.

Immigrants who remained in New York City did not have it any easier. Epidemics of yellow fever and cholera swept through the city. There was famine. The Napoleonic Wars and the War of 1812 caused a practical standstill of both international and domestic shipping and manufacturing. The outbreak of the Civil War exacerbated political strife, economic upheaval, and social maladjustment. There was widespread unemployment, and children as young as five were forced to find ways to keep themselves and sometimes even their families from dying of starvation. In the absence of child welfare laws, a boy could be legally employed at age twelve.

A large floating population of vagrant children coalesced, living on the streets and surviving by their wits. Seldom numbering fewer than ten thousand in any year, they were an illiterate army of orphans and runaways, known as "street Arabs." Almost entirely foreign-born, they were the city's newsboys, bootblacks, flower girls, street sweepers, peddlers, and musicians. Some became gamblers. Others survived by becoming pickpockets, beggars, pimps, and prostitutes.

Newsies

Newsboys—or newsies, as they were called—were a prominent part of the urban landscape of the time. Very young boys, and occasionally girls, hawked their papers for a penny, and represented some of the worst of child labor abuse in the country. In his classic account of New York in the 1870s, the journalist James McCabe wrote, "The newsboys constitute an important division of this army of homeless children. You see them everywhere, in all parts of the city. . . . They rend the air and deafen you with their shrill cries. They are ragged and dirty. Some have no coats, no shoes and no hat."

Newsboys suffered homelessness, harassment, muggings, long hours, and uncertain weather conditions. Newspaper publishers charged fifty cents for a stack of one hundred newspapers and there was no reimbursement for unsold papers. And although reformers tried to help, it was not until the newsboys took action themselves that things began to change. After several publishers raised the cost of a bundle to sixty cents, New York City newsboys went on strike in July 1899. Tying up the city for two weeks, they won a limited victory when the publishers agreed to reimburse them for papers they could not sell. But before their dramatic victory, skirmishes had already occurred in other cities.

On October 14, 1884, the *New York Times* reported one such incident in Pottsville, Pennsylvania, when several newsboys refused to deliver the *Evening Chronicle*. Four newsboys broke ranks, returned to the news office, and picked up their supply of papers, "but as soon as they left the office they were attacked by the strikers and one was severely beaten. The young fellow turned on his assailants and stabbed one in the arm. The proprietors of the *Chronicle* threatened to have the whole party arrested, after which the four boys were allowed to deliver their papers without further trouble. The boys had been getting the paper at sixty cents per one hundred but they wanted it at fifty cents."

Today, homeless adults raise our anxiety level, our guilt, our rage—and sometimes a combination of all three. In the 1850s, homeless children who lived on the street were seen as a threat. There was always talk of placing them in an orphanage, but it remained only talk because there was no place to house them and nobody was willing to pay the enormous sums needed to have orphanages built. Not that these street urchins were likely to have gone willingly, or, for that matter, that they would have stayed. Word on the streets of New York was that orphanages were little more than overcrowded holding pens where children were treated like criminals, marginally clothed and fed, and nominally educated. Why would any streetwise child go to such a place?

Indenturing Children Is "The Answer"

From the 1850s to the 1920s, one "answer" to the problem of helping vulnerable New York children was to have them indentured to farmers and tradesmen, where they would work for a number of years in exchange for food, shelter, and a modicum of education. Archbishop John Hughes of New York was instrumental in founding the Roman Catholic Orphanage Asylum (RCOA) in 1853, with the aim of caring for boys to the age of twelve and girls to the age of fourteen.

"At all events," he announced, "boys over twelve years of age cannot be allowed by me to remain in the Asylum." He had little choice because there simply was no room. Only the youngest could be accommodated in the institution, and the RCOA made the decision to place adolescent boys and girls with tradesmen or families, which often meant "binding out," or indenture.

The Form of Indenture, a contract used by the asylum, stated that "children with neither parent nor guardian living" could be indentured for a specific period of time, during which the child was obligated to perform certain duties. In exchange, the party to whom he or she was indentured was obligated:

> to teach and instruct [the child] in the art, trade, mystery, business and [relevant] occupation of [occupation]. And during all the term aforesaid, the said [tradesman] shall and will allow unto the said [orphan] competent and sufficient meat, drink, and apparel, washing, lodging, mending, and all other things necessary and fit for a [occupation] and shall and will teach and instruct, or cause the said [orphan] to be taught and instructed to read and write, and in so much of arithmetic as is needful for persons in the ordinary ranks of life; and shall give unto the said [orphan] at the expiration of the term of service a new Bible and Prayer Book and a complete suit of new clothing; and shall cause the said individual to attend Divine Worship on Sundays and Holydays [sic] (whenever such attendance is not too inconvenient) during all the term aforesaid and shall not allow the indentured to be absent from the service of the said [tradesman] without express leave, or suffer the [orphan] to haunt ale-houses, taverns, or play-houses, nor at cards, dice, or any unlawful game to play.

Where were New York City children indentured? In 1860, of the fifteen boys from the RCOA who were indentured, two went to saddle and harness makers, four to farmers, two to plumbers, one to a gardener and florist, one to a baker, one to a boot- and shoemaker, one to a rope maker, one to an apothecary, one to a butcher, and one to a dry goods retailer. Of the four girls indentured that same year, one went to a dressmaker, and two were indentured to milliners. One girl was indentured to work in what was called a "fancy store," which today would probably be boutique shop selling luxury merchandise.

The Orphan Train Movement Is "The Answer"

Charles Loring Brace, a reformer of the period, wrote, "I remember one cold night seeing some ten or a dozen of the little homeless creatures piled together to keep each other warm beneath the stairway of *The [New York] Sun* office. There used to be a mass of them at *The Atlas* office, sleeping in the lobbies, until the printers drove them away by pouring water on them."

Brace was a Protestant minister and a reformer who, in 1853, founded the Children's Aid Society. He hated the very idea of the orphanage system, believing that the longer a child remained in the asylum, the less likely he would be to do well in life outside the institution. Brace argued that orphans should be placed in foster care, and he looked west for relatively unexplored vistas. His answer was to ship thousands of orphans out on the "orphan trains" to farms in the Midwest, where they were indentured. Strapping young boys and girls were in great demand. Waiting farmers picked the children they wanted, and often begrudgingly made do with puny substitutes. When the orphan train movement began, it was estimated that thirty thousand abandoned children were living on the streets of New York City. The New York Foundling Hospital also supported the orphan train as a way to help these children. In fact, the orphan train movement is now recognized as the beginning of documented foster care in North America.

While Brace attacked the orphanage system, the orphan train movement was criticized because it did not consider the children's religion when decisions were made about where they should live. And there was no oversight. Children sent halfway across the country were at the mercy of the family that chose them. Siblings were separated, and the luck of the draw determined whether they were treated fairly or abused.

Between its beginning in 1854 and its demise in 1929, an estimated two hundred thousand orphaned, abandoned, and homeless

Asylum Children

A company of children, mostly boys, from the New York Juvenile Asylum, will arrive in Rockford, at the Hotel Holland, Thursday morning, Sept. 6 1888, remaining until evening. They are from 7 to 15 Years of Age [sic].

Homes are wanted for those children with farmers, where they will receive kind treatment and enjoy fair advantages. They have been in the asylum from one to two years, and have received instruction and training preparatory to a term of apprenticeship, and being mostly of respectable parentage, they are desirable children and worthy of good homes.

They may be taken at first upon trial for four weeks, and afterwards, if all parties are satisfied, under indenture—girls until 18 and boys until 21 years of age.

All expenses for transportation will be assumed by the Asylum and the children will be placed on trial and indentured free of charge. The indenture provides for four months schooling each year, until the child has advanced . . . , and at the expiration of the term of apprenticeship, two new suits of clothes, and the payment to the girls of $50 and to the boys of $150. Those who desire to take children on trial are requested to meet them at the hotel at the time above.

children were placed in homes across the United States and Canada. The movement declined dramatically in the 1920s as a growing number of state legislatures began passing laws to restrict or forbid the interstate placement of children. Some states moved even earlier. For example, in 1887, Michigan passed the first law in the United States regulating the placement of children within the state, and in 1895, it passed a state law requiring out-of-state child-placement agencies to post a bond for each child brought into the state. Other states followed. They were less concerned about the children than they were about making sure New York did not export diseased, insane, or criminal youth to their states.

The Orphanage Is "The Answer"

As the United States struggled to come to terms with the terrible losses of human life sustained in the Civil War, fatherless children scavenged for food in the street. Society correctly saw them as victims of the war, and for the first time in U.S. history orphanages were built under public auspices.

On December 5, 1869, the *New York Times* printed a story that tried to explain to its readers what life in an orphanage was like:

> In a City like New York, there are constantly many hundreds of children who are left in destitute circumstances, without parents, and dependent on Public charity for a substitute for a home. The few who are actually adopted into good families are the only ones who know what a real home is. The rest, or such of them as are not left to take the perilous chances of the world or with friends of doubtful character, are cared for in the Orphan Asylums. These are, at best, poor substitutes for home; but in most cases everything is done which can be done by a few teachers and nurses for a collection of a hundred or more children gathered into one establishment.
>
> An orphan asylum is, in fact, a sort of boarding school, with no home to look back or forward to; no holidays or vacations, with delightful visits of parents and friends; but year after year of the strange unnatural school life, to end in most cases with an apprenticeship to a trade, or an indenture to service. Still, the meek Sisters of the Catholic faith, or the kind Protestant teachers and nurses, give the children careful instruction, and their lot is far better than if even these unhomelike [*sic*] homes were not provided for them. . . .
>
> The older girls are taught to sew, and most of the clothing is made in the establishment, while the boys are employed in light

work about the house or the grounds, but seldom taught any regular trade or branch of labor. In fact, they are generally too young for that, being retained in the asylum only until the age of fourteen. On leaving, unless they have friends to whom they may be prudently returned, they are provided with situations, and in most cases indentured until such time as they shall become of age.

3   **The Twentieth Century**

In the twentieth century, the focus shifts from a historical overview of the way things were in the hazy past, with only archival records and yellowed daguerreotypes to guide us, to events and memories that are still fresh because people like me who experienced them are still alive.

Young victims of the Great Depression often wound up at the orphanage gates. Extreme economic hardship created the emotional desperation that drove some wage earners to abandon their familial responsibilities. Parents did not have enough money to keep their children, and as family life disintegrated, adolescents flocked to New York City. Some found their way to orphanages, which became dangerously overcrowded.

World War II created a different kind of crisis for institutions that cared for children. Organizations that had always opened their doors to children whose parents were in difficult circumstances now also had to accommodate the situations that arose when men left home to join the armed forces.

During the war and in the years that immediately followed, the urgent need to find beds for a huge influx of infant baby boomers and young children stretched orphanages to the breaking point. Some were the children of war widows who could not support their family and opted to send one or all of their children to an orphanage for a few years until they remarried or established a way to support them. Others were among the babies born to unmarried women. The U.S. Census Bureau estimated that during World War II and in the years immediately following, there were at least 650,000 out-of-wedlock babies, with the greatest number born between 1943 and 1945. But this official number does not take into account the infants who were not registered as illegitimate, or the mothers who, because of social stigma, invented a husband who had been "killed in combat."

There are no statistics on the number of children made orphans by the war, and there are no studies on the effects their fathers' death had on their lives. More than one soldier, upon learning that his sweetheart was pregnant, abdicated responsibility by getting a superior officer to write a letter claiming that he had died in combat. There are stories of adult children discovering that a father they believed had died a war hero was in actuality alive and well, having abandoned his wife and moved on. One can only imagine the tenor of these family reunions.

Viola Best

The war ended in April 1945. In March 1946, my mother, Viola Best, gave birth to me. I know very little about Viola. She was a poor young woman of German descent who worked in a factory in Brooklyn. She had a boyfriend named Edward Rohs.

My mother had a baby in an environment that was harsh and punitive toward unmarried women like her. American society still judged women on the Victorian values of chastity, self-sacrifice, and family nurturing. Like many women of that era, Viola was poorly educated and possessed few skills. Along with eighteen million others of her sex, she worked in a factory during the war years, filling the temporary labor shortages.

Frequently, women in Viola's situation were shunned by their families. Some mothers gave their children to the orphanage so they could marry without the shame and responsibility that came with being an unwed mother. Some desperate young women left their infants anonymously in baskets provided at the entrance to the New

My mother brought me to the Angel Guardian Home, where I lived for the first two years of my life.

York Foundling Asylum. (Before these baskets appeared in 1869, infanticide was a common crime. Every month, 100–150 dead babies were found in the city, in empty barrels or crates, vacant lots, or floating in the river.) After safe havens were created, the number of abandoned dead babies decreased dramatically, and within three years nearly two thousand babies had been brought to the doors of the Foundling Hospital (see Appendix B).

Sr. Mary Olivera, who worked at Angel Guardian Home the year Viola brought me there, remembers that my mother first tried to manage her difficult situation by having me live with her sister. But that did not work out. Her sister—my aunt—could not manage because she herself was poor. She did not have enough money to feed me properly, and to make matters worse, the boardinghouse where she lived did not allow children. Every time I cried, the poor woman was terrified that the landlord, who lived on the premises, would hear the noise and evict her. My mother visited us every week but did not contribute to my upkeep. It became clear that I could not stay there for long. So, on September 10, when I was six months old, Viola Best and Edward Rohs brought me to the Sisters of Mercy, who were in charge of the Angel Guardian Home for infants. They placed me in the arms of Sr. Olivera of the Sisters of Mercy, under the auspices of the Catholic Church.

My earliest years were lived in two Brooklyn institutions, Angel Guardian Home and Convent of Mercy, and the St. Mary of the Angel Home on Long Island. The Order of the Sisters of Mercy staffed and ran all three homes. Because of the part they played in my early upbringing, and because I am a proud resident of Brooklyn, their history and the history of the institutions they built became part of my history as well.

Raised by the Church

And now abideth faith, hope, charity, these three; but the greatest of these is charity.

1 Corinthians 13:13

4   The Sisters of Mercy: A Tale of Two Cities

In 1846, a small band of nuns from the Order of the Sisters of Mercy made the long and arduous journey from Dublin to New York City. They came after New York's powerful Archbishop John Hughes himself traveled to the Mother House in Dublin specifically to recruit members of their order. Hughes was convinced that young women who came as immigrants to New York were in need of a House of Mercy like that in Dublin, where they could find shelter in a dangerous urban environment. He wanted the house to be for the "women of Ireland arriving in this city, young, pure, innocent, unacquainted with the snares of the world, and the dangers to which poverty and inexperience would expose them in a foreign land."

The Sisters of Mercy who responded to the archbishop's request were young and idealistic. They were the children of wealth and privilege, members of the Irish elite. Their founder, Mother Mary Catherine McAuley, was an orphaned heiress who started the order in Ireland two decades earlier. Their mandate was to continue the work begun in North America by the order's pioneering nun, Mother Frances Xavier Warde, and her six companion sisters, who were working with the poor in Pittsburgh.

The journey from Ireland to New York—which in 1846 took four to six weeks—was daunting. Ships were packed beyond capacity; travelers often suffered from seasickness; and deaths from cholera and typhus were common. Most vessels did not have a doctor aboard.

As soon as they reached shore, the sisters moved into the Convent of Mercy at the corner of Houston and Mulberry Streets in Manhattan. They were profoundly shocked by the illiteracy and lack of cultural sophistication they found among the masses of starving, uneducated immigrants whom they had come to serve. Being upper-class ladies of good breeding, their first project was the establishment of a circulating library of the "great" Catholic works. The books were written in English; the immigrants were illiterate, and even if they could read, most spoke only Gaelic or German. To state it gently, their effort was ineffectual.

But the sisters were a quick study, and by November 1850 they not only understood their challenge but had visited at least eight hundred of the sick and dying poor in their "cellars and garrets." They visited prisoners in the Tombs detention complex twice a week, and opened the convent regularly to the poor, dispensing clothing, shoes, food, and other miscellaneous items. When requested, they also provided religious instruction. The sisters worked closely with the St. Vincent de Paul Society, visiting the city's almshouses and prisons. They founded their own homes for immigrant girls—a halfway house between dependency and work, where the sisters provided spiritual guidance, taught basic skills, and helped women find jobs.

On September 12, 1855, nine years after their arrival in the United States, six Sisters of Mercy left their convent in Manhattan and boarded the ferry for the short trip to Fulton Landing in Brooklyn. They were moving across the river at the urgent bidding of Brooklyn's Bishop John Loughlin, who had requested that the order provide him with sisters to teach at St. James, a new nine-room parish school on Jay Street across from the St. James Cathedral. The school still stands at the corner of Jay and Chapel Streets. It is a simple, three-story red brick building; in 1855, it was one of many low-rise constructions in the immigrant community. Today it exists in sharp contrast to the office buildings and residential skyscrapers that loom over it in a gentrified neighborhood.

The *Brooklyn Eagle,* Brooklyn's local afternoon paper, reported the event on September 28: "A fine residence has been provided for them by the Rt. Rev. Dr. Loughlin, near the cathedral. They will have a large free school under their care, and will attend to the visitation of the sick and the instruction of the ignorant, in accordance with the spirit of their holy rule. In process of time they will hope to establish a House of Mercy adapted to the necessities of the growing Diocese of Brooklyn."

When they arrived, the Order of the Sisters of Mercy came to a young city that seemed in a great hurry to grow up, and 1855 was a banner year. Through consolidation with the cities of Williamsburgh and Bushwick, Brooklyn became the second-largest city in the United States. And on July 6, Walt Whitman quietly made literary history when he offered for sale 795 anonymously written copies of *Leaves of Grass* he had privately published in the Brooklyn Heights print shop of the brothers James and Thomas Rome.

But there was another Brooklyn, and it was to this Brooklyn that Bishop Loughlin had brought the sisters. In 1855, 43 percent of Brooklyn's two hundred thousand residents—eighty-six thousand men, women, and children—were impoverished immigrants who lived in misery. More than 55 percent of that immigrant community was Irish, part of the great exodus from Ireland between 1845 and 1860, when a reported two million people fled the great potato famine. Across the river, New York became known as the largest Irish city in the world, and many of those immigrants spilled over into Brooklyn, living in miserable conditions in the neighborhood known as Vinegar Hill.

Thousands of abandoned Irish children roamed the city streets, and violent gangs brought havoc to their neighborhoods. Prostitution was rampant. (In Manhattan's notorious Five Points alone there were an estimated fifty thousand prostitutes and as many as seventeen brothels.) Many Irish immigrants communicated in their own street slang known as "flash talk," which further alienated them from the outside world. (Some flash talk stuck; for example, the expression "going on a bender," which was flash talk for a drinking binge, is today an accepted colloquial expression.) Irish prostitutes, known in flash talk as "nymphs of the pave," walked the Brooklyn streets, and illegitimacy reached stratospheric heights.

The vast majority of social welfare institutions at the time were sponsored by religious organizations. Catholic dioceses founded scores of caretaking institutions, including schools, hospitals, and homes for the aged, infants and unwed mothers, and workingwomen. Through their commitment to working with the poorest and most vulnerable, the Sisters of Mercy would become part of Brooklyn's historic human treasure. But in 1855, they were already part of the national fabric.

Ten years before their arrival in Brooklyn, small notices regarding the sisters began to appear on the pages of the *Brooklyn Eagle.* The *Eagle* archives provide a window into the growing influence of the sisters and their participation in the local community. The paper first mentions the Sisters of Mercy in the United States on August 12, 1845, under the heading "The Veil": "On Monday, at St. Paul's Cathedral, Pittsburg, Pa, Miss Eliza Wynne (Sister Mary Catherine) and Miss E. McCaffrey (Sister Mary Agnes) received the White Veil in the Order of Sisters of Mercy from the Rt. Reverend Bishop."

Other articles began to appear with greater frequency. They provide a glimpse into a time not so long ago yet light-years away.

> *June 16, 1849*: "The 'St. Catherine's Convent of the Sisters of Mercy' situated in Houston Street between Mulberry and Broadway was about [to receive] an enlargement . . . a plain brick building, three stories high . . . and will cost some $14,000–$16,000."
>
> *August 25, 1854*: "The Yellow Fever at New Orleans appears to be on the increase. The Sisters of Mercy have closed their schools and will hereafter devote their entire attention to administering to the wants of the sick."

The Sisters of Mercy cared for me from ages two to six at the Convent of Mercy.

August 8, 1855: "The Sisters of Mercy have notified the friends of Miss Oatman, the young lady recently rescued from the Indians, that they will receive her into their care."

August 23, 1859: "Melancholy Casualty: A Sister of Mercy Killed. We are pained to record an accident of a most melancholy nature which transpired on Saturday afternoon, near the residence of Chauncey Brooks, Esq., Charles Street, resulting in the death of a Sister Cipriani, a most estimable and beloved member of the charitable Order of the Sisters of Mercy, and for seven years the efficient matron of Mount Hope Insane Asylum. The facts of the occurrence, as nearly as we could collect them, show that the unfortunate Sister, having some business to transact a few miles from Mount Hope, was being driven to the place by a man connected with the Mount Hope farm, when the horse taking fright dashed off at a furious rate. Sister Cipriani, exhibiting some alarm, was requested by the driver to retain her seat; and the frightened animal requiring all of his skill and attention, the driver did not again notice the Sister until he had finally succeeded in checking the animal's career [sic], and when he turned he discovered her suspended by her clothing from the rear of the vehicle, her head touching the ground and horribly fractured—a position in which probably she had been dragged during the entire course run by the animal, a distance of nearly two miles. She was entirely dead when discovered."

April 24, 1889: "Tuberculosis was said to have broken out among the three cows at the convent of the Sisters of Mercy, Classon and Willoughby Avenue. The Health Department has been notified. At the Convent it was found that the outbreak was not serious."

Within a year, the school on Jay Street became a resource for orphans who lived on the street. Seven years later, in November 1862, the sisters and their young charges moved to the Convent of Mercy, a magnificent new convent residence and orphanage complex at 237 Willoughby Avenue designed by Patrick Keely, the most important Catholic architect in the country. For more than a hundred years after its construction, the order would raise hundreds of thousands of children within its cloistered walls.

5

My Earliest Years

Angel Guardian Home
12th Avenue and 63rd Street
Brooklyn, New York
(My home, 1946–48)

Convent of Mercy
273 Willoughby Avenue
Brooklyn, New York
(My home, 1948–52)

The Angel Guardian Home was one of the many institutions for children founded by the Sisters of Mercy. When it opened in 1899, the first residents were ninety girls, ages two to five, who had been separated from their families for all the reasons children ended up in such places—a parent got sick and could not handle taking care of children; or they lost their home; or they were just too poor to manage.

Boys were accepted in 1903, and in 1906 the sisters commissioned the nursery where I was placed. That same year Angel Guardian began placing children with families in the community. During the Great Depression, eight nuns took care of 185 young boys. From what I remember of those energetic and spirited sisters, I know that they were up to the task. Today Angel Guardian provides foster care and runs programs that facilitate adoption and the reunification of biological families.

"After taking my vows," Sr. Mary Johanna, S.M., recalled, "I was sent to work in Angel Guardian Home in the nursery. In those years, it was customary for one-year-olds to be moved from the infant quarters to another area of the institution that had been set aside for older infants. That nursery was called St. Joseph's. But in 1947 there was such an influx of orphans in postwar America that we couldn't accommodate all the older orphans and so, Eddie, you had to stay in the nursery for the newborns for an additional six months. St. Joseph's was packed and we just didn't have the room to move you. I cared for fourteen infants in the nursery. There were four wards in addition to the mothers who came for prenatal training. After they gave birth to their babies there was a ward awaiting them, making it five. Across the yard we had three wards of babies who had to be potty trained. There were at least sixty boys in that unit, with a lot of people helping out.

"When you turned two, they moved you to the Convent of Mercy in Fort Greene, where the older little boys lived. A couple of months later I was transferred there myself. To tell you the truth, Eddie, I didn't want to go. I liked being with my newborn babies, and when they sent me over to Mercy I wasn't at all happy. But you know, when the mother superior of the order makes a decision we are required to follow, with no questions asked.

"As soon as I arrived I went looking for you, Eddie, and when I finally found you I could tell right away that the move had had a bad effect. When I sent you over you were a fat little baby with a big smile. Now you were undernourished and listless. I began to understand that it was God's will that I was transferred. I was there to help you get back on your feet."

I will never fully understand why, one day, out of the blue, I decide to call the Angel Guardian Home and ask for my case records. After I submit a formal request and go through bureaucratic process, a social worker calls, and with the speed (and sensitivity) of a machine gun, she begins rattling off information about my earliest history. She speaks so rapidly and says so much that is unfamiliar and upsetting to me that I must to ask her to stop so I can get a pen and pad

Sister Mary Johanna is on the right.

to write it all down. And then I have to beg her to please, please slow down!

The story she presents is worse than anything I could have imagined. She says that after one week of confinement my mother took me to her sister, who lived in a one-room studio apartment in the Greenpoint section of Brooklyn. The landlord did not allow children. According to the records, my parents wanted to abort me because my father was already married to someone else and had two children, a boy Billy and a girl named Dotty, but they could not afford the procedure.

I control my impulse to hang up on her because there is more. Apparently, my mother visited every week but brought no food or money to help my aunt care for me. Six months after I was born my aunt told her sister Viola that she had to take me back. And that is when my mother brought me to the orphanage. Then, a couple of years ago, I had a chance meeting with a Sister of Mercy who remembered caring for me when I arrived at Angel Guardian. She filled in more of my story. I was a sickly and malnourished infant, which would make sense given the information the social worker had provided about my life in my aunt's boarding house. The Angel Guardian Home required that my mother stay with me for at least a week and participate in the Angel Guardian mother-child reunification program, which was designed to encourage a bond between a mother and her newborn. Reuniting a mother with her child was the Christian thing to do; but the sister also admitted that in 1946 the orphanage was filled beyond capacity with infants. They were desperate for mothers to fall in love with their newborns and take them home. But in my case it did not happen; Viola could not be convinced. And so, after a week, the Sisters of Mercy had no choice but to take over. And take over they did. When I arrived I was sickly and malnourished, but the sister recalled that eight months later I was strong enough to climb over the crib rails. She remarked that the sisters were overjoyed because their prayers had been answered.

I am overwhelmed by sadness and anger. I can never forgive my mother for giving me up so easily, and for never coming back after she was settled. For never visiting or sending me a birthday card. For never signing the papers that would release me for adoption. For never caring enough. For never caring.

On a blustery February morning, Judith and Steve Estrine, Elsie Pascrell, and I went to visit the various homes I have lived in. Our first stop was the Angel Guardian Home. We were graciously received,

Convent of Mercy Closes

After 146 years of service ministering to the community, the Sisters of Mercy closed their Convent of Mercy in 2010. Dwindling numbers of sisters in the Brooklyn diocese necessitated that they merge with the mid-Atlantic Order in Merion, Pennsylvania. They lost autonomy, and the decision to close the Convent of Mercy was made by the new leadership, who cited the prohibitive cost (more than $24 million) of fixing the old building's serious structural and accessibility problems to meet the City of New York's new safety standards. According to Sister Francene Horan, "It kind of hurts in a lot of ways. A building was one thing. This was a home, the place you knew would give you a place to stay. It's like saying your parents died and you don't have a home anymore." Sister Francene came to the motherhouse in the 1950s to teach kindergarten.

but it was clear that the orphanage where Viola dropped me off and where I lived for a year no longer exists. And when I told the young sister who was showing us around about my relationship to their institution, she began treating me like an artifact from a bygone era. Which I guess I am.

Our next stop was the Convent of Mercy, where the Sisters of Mercy and the hundreds of children in their care moved in November 1862. Again, we were received graciously and Sister Aquinas showed us around the beautiful building, with its inlaid Italian wood and marble designs. I was very moved to enter once again the chapel where, early in my life, I first heard the Sisters of Mercy sing.

Several months later, on another cold and overcast afternoon in early November, Judith and I drove to Hicksville, New York, out on Long Island, where Sr. Mary Johanna and nineteen other older Sisters of Mercy lived in a compact two-story convent adjoining the school where for many years she taught Spanish.

When I opened the car door, I was hit with a biting wind. It crossed my mind to ask Sister if she would be happier in a warmer climate. Surely there must be Sisters of Mercy convents for retired nuns in Arizona or Florida. When I mentioned it later, she brushed it off. She liked living here among her friends and colleagues. This was her home.

Johanna was waiting for us in the simple visiting room off the community area, where the sisters read and watched television, and the dining room, where a full-time cook served their meals. (A couple of years ago, she requested that I stop calling her by her formal religious name, which was Sister Mary Johanna. It was easy for me to drop the name "Mary" that all sisters took upon entering her order, but to this day I continue to call her "Sister Johanna.")

It was a room of subtle mauves and tans—a peaceful space. As usual, I was all nervous energy. At eighty-nine, Johanna radiated a more measured but still youthful enthusiasm. When I was a boy, Johanna always wore a long flowing robe with wide long sleeves and close-fitting under-sleeves of the same fabric. She wore a belt that some nuns used as an instrument to discipline the kids, although I never saw her use it on anyone. Her veil was also long and black. The only contrast was a white starched linen headdress that completely covered her hair and ears, and left only her eyes, nose, mouth, and cheeks uncovered. Her collar was also made of very stiff white linen and covered her chest. She wore black stockings and black leather shoes—and, of course, her rosary beads. I always knew when Sister Johanna or one of the other nuns was nearby due to the sound of their beads clanking as they walked. When I lived at the Convent of Mercy, Johanna seemed ethereal, and never more so than when she and other nuns were in the chapel for Sunday Mass, singing their prayers a cappella, filling the chapel with glorious song.

On the afternoon we met, she was dressed for the occasion in a pink flowered leisure suit, her snow-white hair recently given a perm. The only way a stranger would know she was a nun was by the cross she wore around her neck. She seated us at the maple wood table adorned with simple plastic doilies.

"So how are you, Eddie? How's the book coming?"

I told her about the institutions we had already visited and the people we had interviewed. I asked for her help in fleshing out my first years and she plunged into the story with gusto. Listening to her describe her experiences in 1946 with an inflection that was pure Brooklyn Irish, I was brought back in time to my youth and overcome by a kind of sweet sadness. I was also learning about things that I had never heard from anybody before. Judith and Sister Johanna were on a roll, and we were all having fun.

How Johanna Came to Be a Sister of Mercy

"My parents came from Ireland," Johanna remembers, "and they were married there. My oldest brother was born and died there, and when my second brother was about a year old, they came over and settled in Brooklyn. My father got a job with Brooklyn Rapid Transit—BRT. It was a terrible job—he worked all day, sometimes seven days a week, ten hours a day, with no vacation. If he was late to work, he was docked. It was terrible.

"So some of the men—all Irish immigrants like my father—agitated for better conditions and some things were done. But one of them, a widow with a little girl, lost her job as a ticket agent. They went on strike to support her and they were all blacklisted.

"Dad was out of work with a family to support and so he worked as a handyman. He was a very good carpenter. Then he raised pedigree Airedale puppies. He built a big shed across the backyard and that's where he kept them. It took away part of the yard but then they had space to walk around. He made enough money from those dogs to buy a house in Bay Ridge, Brooklyn, and a few years after that he bought another house because he figured the income from renting one would be enough to keep us going, and he was right. As a kid, I never even knew there was a depression because we never wanted for anything.

Sr. Johanna as a novitiate in back row standing on the right.

"In 1937, the BRT was finally unionized. I remember the man who lived upstairs was working as an electrician for BRT, and when he came and told my father, you'd think the man had been given a million dollars, he was that happy.

"Yes, we were union people. My brother worked for the telephone company, and they tried to label the workers who struck as communists. But the judge ruled in the workers' favor and they finally got a union, too. When my brother came to visit me, he grinned

Sr. Johanna's Christmas Story

"The Convent of Mercy was near the Brooklyn Navy Yard and when the ships returned after World War II they were put in dry dock, among them the *Aris*. Near Christmastime in 1952—which was the last year Eddie was with us—the chaplain of the *Aris* called and invited us all to come on board for a Christmas Day celebration. So we arranged for two buses to take the boys to the ship along with the lay teachers who worked with them and some of the sisters. Quite an exciting expedition. When the boys woke up and saw their good clothes on the bed, they knew it meant that they were going out and then it was all excitement. That morning we had no trouble getting them to eat breakfast.

"At the assigned time they were all ready and running around the vestibule in their snowsuits. We waited and waited but no bus came, and finally Sister Josephus went to the office and called the man who ran the bus company. He couldn't believe what he was hearing.

"'Sister, haven't you looked out the window? There's a blizzard out there. I didn't risk sending my drivers out—no way—no way.' Oh dear. We had promised ninety-three little boys a special outing, and instead we had to get everyone upstairs and tell them that the event was cancelled. Well, we could say what we wanted, but the boys weren't taking off their snowsuits. They had been promised a treat. Talk about a rebellion!

"In desperation Sr. Consuelo broke down and pulled out the box of candy canes her mother had sent for the boys and that she was saving to give as a special treat, and used them instead to bribe the boys to stop their insurrection and get into play clothes.

"So now everything was going fine. The boys were in their play clothes, hands smeared with candy cane. Then a couple of sailors appeared at the door and Sister Josephus came running in with the

(*continued*)

Sr. Johanna's Christmas Story (*continued*)

announcement, 'Put the snowsuits on, they're coming up in private cars from the Navy Yard.' Now to get the candy canes out of ninety-three pairs of little hands, clean several hundred sticky fingers, put the holiday clothes back on and zip up the snowsuits of ninety-three little boys with candy-smeared faces and pockets filled with contraband candy that they had refused to relinquish.

"Well, we finally got down to the *Aris* and learned that the shipmates had invited nine orphanages of all denominations to come that day from Brooklyn and Queens, but because of the weather none could make it except us, because we were close to the Navy Yard.

"Each of our boys had his own personal sailor to show him around, and at the end of the day every one of them received a huge shopping bag with nice clothes, good toys, and a big red stocking. But the gift I will always remember was a little T-shirt with the USS *Aris* insignia. Those shirts were indestructible. They lasted for years and years and years. When a boy outgrew it, we gave it to a younger child. We actually grew sick and tired of them and grumbled to each other, 'Why don't they wear out like normal clothes?' But no one at the convent could bear to throw out anything that was still good, and those navy-issue shirts were extremely good. Several years later, I read that the government was destroying old World War II ships. The first one to go was the *Aris*. But the memory of that great ship lived on in those little T-shirts, worn year in, year out, by generations of little boys."

and announced, 'Johanna, you'll be glad to hear your brother is not a communist.'

"I worked as a secretary for three years after graduating from Bishop McDonnell Memorial High School in 1938 before I entered the order. My dad didn't want me to become a nun, but I persevered, and he finally told me he would give me his blessing if I waited until I was twenty-one. I think he hoped I would find a nice young man and marry by then, but when he died when I was twenty, my mother took me aside and told me I could join the order if that was what I really wanted. And I told her it was what I really and truly wanted, so I did."

My Aunt Katherine

When I was four years old, people in the community held a Halloween party at the Convent of Mercy where I lived. It was at this party that I met a woman who had a profound influence on my life for years to come. It was one of those lively, raucous, chaotic events the neighborhood used to throw for orphans, with sticky candy and butter-cream-frosted cupcakes and lots of pushing and shoving. Parenthetically, these parties stopped when we entered the surly, prepubescent phase of human development—in short, when we stopped being small and cute. But while we were little, it was a good way for the church community to do a good deed while at the same time teaching their offspring how lucky they were to have parents who loved them.

Everyone showed up—neighborhood kids, their mothers, kindly churchwomen who came to volunteer. And of course the sisters, who tried to keep some degree of order and prevent eyes from being poked out by the apples on sticks the neighborhood Cub Scouts had brought. In the middle of all the noise, the crying, and the pushing I spotted a beautiful, glamorous lady with red lipstick and nails to match, smoking a cigarette. Nobody was paying her the slightest bit of attention, but I marched right up and announced, "My name is Eddie Rohs. Who are you?"

"My name is Katherine McCarthy. I'm Sr. Mary Johanna's sister. I'm glad to meet you, Eddie."

Being just four years old, I was overcome by the enormity of what I had just done, and I ran away. But a seed was planted. She became my "Aunt" Katherine. And although for years I did not even understand what being an "aunt" meant, I understood that, more than any other adult I knew, she made me feel like I was worth caring about.

6 St. Mary of the Angel

Convent Road
Syosset, New York

In my day at St. Mary's, it was a complete farm. We, as summer arrived, helped in the many little tasks—the chickens, the gathering of the eggs, feeding the pigs; in the fall the picking of the fruit, the vegetables and helping to store them to better enjoy them during the long winter months. As we matured, we got our own little garden patch, prepared the soil, to plant, to pick, and yes to eat. . . . In the St. Mary of my day, we all played together, fought together, shared our hurts, our gifts and at times cried together. And it was good.

From a letter by Francis Spearman to Sr. Mary Sean,
reprinted in *One Hundred Years of Mercy*

A Summer Home

I came to live at St. Mary of the Angel in 1952. It had the feel of a rustic homestead, although in fact it was an institution that housed 172 boys in three dormitories. The property, a 120-acre farm in Syosset, Long Island, had belonged to the Van Nostrand family. The church purchased it in 1893 for $7,500, in order to use it as a summer retreat for the Brooklyn's Convent of Mercy sisters, and for children suffering from respiratory problems. The following year the property was given the name St. Mary of the Angel.

The sisters and the older boys managed the farm, where fresh vegetables were grown for everyone who stayed there; produce was

St. Mary of the Angel in Syosset, New York, was my home between ages six and eleven.

shipped to the sisters and children who remained at the convent in Brooklyn, and the surplus was sold to the community for income. Before long, St. Mary's evolved into a year-round residence for orphans, and in 1905 a school for the younger boys was built, although older boys attended local schools.

First Memories

I have wisps and pieces of memory of my years at St. Mary's. It was rural but there was a nearby town with its one general store, and I remember the delicious candy and ice cream it sold. Community organizations like the American Legion, Elks Club, Knights of Columbus, Rotary Club, and the police and fire fraternal organizations, proudly wearing their impressive uniforms, sponsored parties for us. And when they were not bringing gaiety into St. Mary's, they were taking us out—to Jones Beach, Madison Square Garden, Yankee and

On my birthdays I received elegantly wrapped cookies from Aunt Katherine purchased at Brooklyn's Abraham & Straus department store. I taunted the other kids: "Ha! Ha! Look at what I got from my Aunt Katherine. They're mine and you can't have any." The nun in charge of the playground chided me: "Ed Rohs, aren't you going to share your cookies with the other kids?" My response was always, "My Aunt Katherine bought them for me, for my birthday."

Shea Stadiums—in the institution's purple bus. At these events we sat way in back so it was nearly impossible see anything. But it was a treat just to leave the orphanage! The only sad part was that no one had money and we could only stare longingly at spectators who wolfed down their popcorn, hot dogs, and Cracker Jacks.

I have pictures of a solemn May Day procession. Participants included all 172 boys, the nuns, and the new novitiates from the nearby Mercy Academy, a private Catholic high school for girls. Every year, one of the St. Mary's boys was chosen to lead the procession to the front of the institution. One year I was given the honor and got to carry the crown of flowers to the grotto, which featured a stature of the Blessed Virgin Mary.

And I have a memory of embarrassing one of the nuns during an assembly performance. I was on the stage with the other boys and I raised my hand. The sister ignored me. I raised it again, this time expressing more urgency. She turned away. Finally, in desperation I called out, "Sister, please," and she snapped, "What is it, Ed?" I blurted out, "I have to go to the bathroom, Sister." The audience roared and the sister, her face burning with fury, dragged me off the stage. Ten minutes later, the audience acknowledged my return with a thunderous round of applause.

Of course I will never forget early mornings at the home! Three sisters were responsible for more than eighty energetic boys in a dormitory,

Leading the procession and carrying the crown of flowers.

and stern discipline was the only way they could keep order. The Hollywood image of genial priests and ethereal nuns was a myth. Life in St. Mary's was ordered, disciplined, and relentlessly efficient.

Typically, on weekday morning Srs. Mary Olivera and Mary Joseph marched up and down the dormitory aisles, black habits rus-

Me and some community girls at St. Mary's.

tling against the checkered tile floors, yelling like drill sergeants, "Up and at 'em! Up and at 'em!" Barefoot and half blind, I would stumble down the long, narrow, institutional green dorm to the shower room. Friends, wide awake and overflowing with life, screamed for the pleasure of hearing their voices compete with the deafening roar of multiple showers going full blast. Stripping out of my rumpled blue striped pajamas, I waited on line until a kid, naked and dripping wet, came bounding out of a stall.

Then it was my turn. I would stand under the showerhead as blasts of hot water snapped me into the day. Soaping up with a bar of Ivory soap and running the white terry cloth washcloth around my neck and ears, I sometimes took a moment to watch as the water washed soapy suds down the drain. Then it was back to business. I brushed my teeth with a clear plastic Colgate toothbrush—an exact replica of the toothbrush owned by every other kid in the place— ran a towel through my G.I. Joe haircut, wrapped a towel around my waist, and raced back to bed.

Grabbing the folded clothes Sr. Mary Joseph always left on my chair, I dove under the covers until I was completely covered—face, torso, butt. The only visible parts of my anatomy were my pink, damp feet. My aim was twofold. First, I had to get dressed as quickly as possible so as not to be late for breakfast. Under the covers, I pulled off the towel and struggled into underpants, khaki shorts, and a blue T-shirt. Second, and of equal if not greater importance, I aimed to spare Sr. Mary Joseph the unpleasantness of seeing me naked. Since early childhood, every boy had it drummed into him that the sisters must not see him unclothed.

Dressed and nearly ready to go, I jammed my stocking feet into white-and-black Converse sneakers and laced them up tight. I made my bed with sharp hospital corners, as I had been taught, and ran to the spot where, each morning, Sr. Joseph assembled my group of thirty-five ten-year-olds for our assault on the dining room. And every morning we would enter just as the previous group was leaving.

"In the name of the Father, and of the Son, and of the Holy Ghost, bless this food we are about to eat . . . " Amen. Then it was all about the food and the ticking clock because we had only fifteen minutes before we were thrown out and the next group entered. We consumed hard-boiled eggs and day-old Wonder bread, orange juice poured from #10 institutional black Sysco cans, and milk from plastic gallon pitchers. Most of what we ate was government surplus, but we boys did not know about that and we probably wouldn't have cared if we did.

Like all institutional meals at the time, the place settings were made of durable plastic green or tan dinner plates, bowls, bread and dessert plates, and clear plastic glasses. Our vegetables and fruits came from institutional #10 size cans, and I got to open them when I helped set the tables. The vegetables were string beans, carrots, corn, peas, or mixed vegetables. The fruits were always pears, red plums, peaches, or mixed fruits, and there was a plentiful supply of government-surplus cheese, butter, rice, and sugar. If we misbehaved we were punished, and if we did not eat quickly we did not get a second chance for a meal. Fussy eaters did not exist and requests for seconds were unheard of. Nobody ever starved, but neither were we ever full;

my friends and I kept trying to break into the huge, padlocked institutional refrigerators between meals. We never succeeded, but that did not stop us from trying.

The Grimmers

By the time I turn six, I know that something is amiss and that I am different from the boys in the community who come to church every Sunday and pay dutiful visits to the orphanage with their parents on holidays, bearing toys and cakes. I dream of being rescued, and I am not alone. I think everyone dreams of leaving the institution, and a few lucky boys actually do. A few are adopted and some go to live in foster care—"boarding out," as it was then called. Occasionally a child's parents take him home. In my heart of hearts, I wish that Aunt Katherine would take me to live with her, but it never happens. She comes to visit and there are gifts and cards, but she never invites me to come live with her in her mansion on the hill.

One summer day, shortly after my eighth birthday, the Grimmer family, who know me from the Holy Family Roman Catholic Church in Hicksville where we all go to pray, asks the sisters if they can take me into their home for a couple of weeks on a trial visit. It is only three blocks away from the church and I have already been there for a day visit. Since they have a newborn baby of their own, I figure they must really love kids. It is an experiment to see if we click. If we do, they will formally request that I move in with them as a boarding child, to become part of the family, to share holidays and vacations, eat their food, attend either a public school or Catholic grammar school in the local community. In short, if it all works out I will enjoy all the rights and privileges given to a son.

The sisters are overjoyed for several reasons. As you know, I cannot be formally adopted because my parents have never legally given up their parental rights—at any point, they could, legally, come back and get me. But neither can the sisters put me on a waiting list of boys suitable for foster care because, when I was only two, I received a low score on a primitive pediatric IQ test that was state of the art—for 1948. The test, which measured the speed with which a young child responded to visual cues, doomed dreamy kids like me to the status of borderline retarded. The Grimmers, it would seem, are a gift from God.

The Grimmers are a nice couple, and the sisters have been pushing them on me for a while now: "It would be so nice, Eddie, if . . ." They live in a typical single-family house of the era, one of the Levittown homes on Long Island built right after World War II for returning veterans. It is a brand-new development and the Grimmers' home is on Nargin Court—in fact, it is so new that no trees have even been planted yet. Mr. Grimmer is a strict man. At our very first meeting, he tells me that if I expect to find a vacation from rules and regulations, I have come to the wrong place. Although he never lays a hand on me, the environment feels harsh.

Mr. Grimmer works for Canada Dry as a salesman and travels to all the supermarkets and delicatessens in Nassau and Suffolk Counties. After I move in, I get to drink tons of soda! For a couple of days after arriving there I feel like the luckiest kid in the world, but then I tire of ginger ale. The stuff is coming out of my ears, but I am afraid to say anything and besides, I have been taught to eat and be appreciative of whatever food I get. (To this day, I cannot stand ginger ale!)

I stay with the Grimmers for two weeks, and they try their best to make me feel at home. I learn to ride a bike in their driveway and in the cul-de-sac at the end of the street. I play with neighborhood kids and, in an early attempt to deinstitutionalize myself, I try emulating how they talk, how they walk, and how they play. I eat delicious home-cooked meals for the first time in my young life, and I see what a family does on weekends.

I sleep in my own room. It is a perfectly acceptable boy's room, but it is the very normalcy of this private space, separated from others, that presents a big problem. How can I explain to them—or to anyone for that matter—that I miss the security of sleeping in a dormitory with other boys? How can I tell them that I am frightened and lonely, and that the privacy they are giving me is creepy?

Mrs. Grimmer takes me shopping to a supermarket. There I discover Technicolor pyramids of fruit, fresh green beans and pea-pods overflowing their bins, red mesh bags of potatoes and onions, and dewy iceberg lettuce and tomatoes so crimson I am sure they are not real. And that's just the produce section. As Mrs. Grimmer walks from aisle to aisle, I watch her choose from a variety of breads available in the bakery section and cheeses from the dairy. And not just American cheese! That is available, of course, but there is also Muenster, cheddar, cream, and Swiss cheese. To say nothing of meat and ice cream and cookies and cakes . . . this is abundance the likes of which I have never seen, and choices I never knew existed. Mrs. Grimmer just keeps piling more and more items into her shopping cart, like she is planning to feed an army.

I whisper, "What's this for?" and "Why are you buying that?" I can tell she does not know why I am asking her about things that are just commonplace grocery items. When we get to the aisle devoted to cereals, Mrs. Grimmer kindly asks me, "Do you prefer Kellogg's Corn Flakes, Krinkles, or Rice Krispies?" I am speechless. Nobody has ever asked me that question because at the home I have to eat whatever is given to me: corn flakes in summer and oatmeal in winter.

The Grimmers take me to a barbershop and to Gertz department store, where they buy me my first Easter outfit. Again, Mrs. Grimmer asks me to choose which suit I prefer, but I cannot for the life of me decide. How can I choose between the brown suit and the blue tweed when I have always gotten all my clothes from the laundry room in the basement? I finally choose the brown suit because everyone is waiting impatiently for an answer. Before the Grimmers, I was never in a supermarket or a department store. As for the barbershop, all I know is that a local barber from town comes to St. Mary's every couple of weeks, equipped with clippers, scissors, and a barber's apron. We all line up in the gym and wait for him to give us a haircut that takes no more than three minutes. We receive the exact same haircut because a nun is always there, instructing him what to do. Getting individual attention in a proper barbershop is an unheard-of luxury.

The Grimmer family has no idea that prior to my visit with them, nobody has ever provided me with the experiences they take for granted. I have no idea what it is like to window-shop, or even browse. Why would I, when the institution takes care of everything? I have never been asked to decide anything. In short, by the time I go to live with the Grimmers, I am totally institutionalized.

I count the days until Mr. Grimmer drives me back. I want no part of living in a house with a man who frightens me. I do not like sleeping alone and I am not comfortable playing with the neighborhood boys. I miss my friends. Give me the institution with dozens of orphaned and abandoned boys any day. When I return to the home the nuns

My theatrical debut at St. Mary of the Angel. (I'm at the far right.)

St. Mary of the Angel. I'm in the first row, leaning in from the left.

are all over me, wanting to hear about my experience. Was I happy there? Did I think I could live there? The Grimmers have already told the sisters they want me to join their family as a foster child. But it ends there. Nothing ever happens. Quietly and without saying much, I let the sisters know that I am happier living with them. They never raise the issue again.

Fifty-five years later, over coffee, I tell Sister Johanna why I never went to live with the Grimmers and we reminisce about that little boy and the choices he made so long ago.

Sister Annunciata

What I remember most about my years at St. Mary of the Angel were the nuns, and of all the nuns who cared for me, I remember

Sister Mary Annunciata with special fondness. She was in the same order and wore the exact same habit as Sr. Johanna, but she was a different kind of nun. Sister Johanna was young and stately, stern and serene, with blue eyes and a crisp habit. I never saw Sr. Johanna's hair because in those years, before Vatican II decreed that sisters could dress modestly in street clothes, we were not allowed to see a nun's hair at all. I was in awe of Sr. Johanna. She was cool and composed and always in control. Sr. Johanna was my personal Virgin Mary.

Sr. Annunciata was a lot older and very robust. Wisps of her dark brown hair were always escaping from under the wimple to her cheek, or hanging from her damp forehead until, with a look of exasperation, she tucked the wayward strand back in place, where it would stay put for a while before creeping out again. And she perspired a lot, especially in summer, when she would mop herself with a white handkerchief she pulled out from under her sleeve. In short, while Sr. Johanna seemed ethereal, Sr. Annunciata was all too human. But when I think of her, I remember a nun who was downright jolly. Sr. Annunciata bubbled over with the simple pleasure of being alive. The dormitory she supervised was as well run and disciplined as any, but when Sr. Annunciata sat down to take a break, kids came out of the woodwork to hang onto her arms and sit in her lap. She was maternal and loving, and when I was with her I was happy.

Kevin the Monster

Every day after school we went back to our dormitory and changed into play clothes. If weather permitted, the nuns would drop us off in the playground, and on rainy days in the playroom, which was located in the basement under the kitchen. Kevin was a lay counselor whom the sisters hired to supervise us kids during playtime. He was a stocky blond, with blue eyes and hairy forearms. Kevin always looked neat and preppy in his khaki pants and short-sleeved, button-down plaid shirts and dress shoes. And so innocent. I guess that is why the sisters trusted him and never came down to see what he was up to. Unfortunately, when their backs were turned, Kevin was up to a great deal.

What the sisters did not know was that Kevin was a sadist who always found some excuse to discipline us. For the slightest infraction we were forced to hang from the rafters by our hands, and when we fell to the floor from the pain he hit our fingers, picked us up, and made us hang some more. He scared the heck out of me, but I believed it was his right to demand that I hang from the pipes and get hit for misbehaving. I also did not question his right to punish us by making us face the wall with our pants and underpants pulled down below our knees while he conducted "inspections." But even though I hated Kevin and thought him cruel and mean, nobody ever told me his behavior was out of bounds. And even if I had known, to whom could I go to report him? In those years, I never thought anyone would believe me, a little kid, over an adult like Kevin.

Today, friends are disturbed when I tell my story about Kevin in a matter-of-fact manner. What about the trauma? Where is the rage? The truth is that I experienced plenty of both, and to this day I bear scars that will never disappear. But these memories are wrapped within the larger context of the trauma I experienced as a child being raised in an environment that lacked sufficient staff trained to listen and respond to me. Think about it: two adult women were responsible for the care of fifty little boys. In that context, Kevin was only the most shocking and outrageous of many difficult situations that were out of my control.

Someone recently told me that shortly after I left St. Mary's Kevin was relieved of his childcare duties and transferred to a job as chauffeur for the sisters with no direct contact with the boys of St. Mary's. I salute the whistle-blower. I only wish it had happened sooner.

Homes for Boys

Home is the place where,
When you have to go there,
They have to take you in.

Robert Frost, *The Death of the Hired Man*

7

St. John's Home for Boys

144 BEACH 111TH STREET
ROCKAWAY PARK, NEW YORK

In the latter half of the nineteenth century, St. John's was the name given to the institution for boys that opened near Albany and Troy Avenues in Brooklyn. At its peak, the Sisters of St. Joseph cared for about a thousand boys, but in 1937, at the request of Bishop Thomas Molloy of Brooklyn, the Marianist Brothers took over responsibility for the program. Coinciding with the decrease in the number of boys coming to the institution, the City of New York, exercising eminent domain, vacated the home to build a large city housing project for low-income families.

St. John's Home for Boys bought property in Rockaway Park in Queens. Rockaway was a beach community and vacation spot when the diocese purchased land there from the Hebrew Home for Convalescent Children on Beach 111th Street. Boys being cared for in St. Malachy's Home in the adjacent Beach 112th Street (now the site of Stella Maris High School) were transferred there as well.

Moving Day

On September 6, 1956, I was transferred from St. Mary of the Angels Home for Boys in Syosset to St. John's Home for Boys in Rockaway Park. I was eleven years old. Although years later I learned that the

I lived with the Marianist Brothers at St. John's Home between ages eleven and fourteen.

nuns had done their best to get me ready for the move, I remember nothing about the weeks preceding that final morning. All I recall is that when I left I was angry and powerless to prevent my leaving St. Mary's. As the bus pulled out, I stared out the window as the suburban green turned into tan inner-city houses crammed one next to the other.

My first glimpse of St. John's Home for Boys (SJH) did nothing to lift my spirits. To my child's eyes, this new home was huge—a long, four-story red brick building that took up half a city block. Adjacent to it was a large, white-shingle-clapboard school building and a very large playground area. (I learned later that the large building comprised dormitories, a recreation room, dining room, kitchen, laundry room, chapel, religious brothers' quarters, infirmary, band room, and canteen.)

Clutching my black garbage bag, I went with Brother August, the director, to a large, open dormitory where, like all the homes I had been to before, my only furnishings were a bed and locker.

"In those days, Eddie, " remembers Sister Olivera, "we didn't know what we know now. Nobody in those days was trained to deal with young boys who were about to be uprooted from an environment where they had been raised by nuns and moved to a home where their only superiors were brothers. Besides, there were too many boys in each dorm and they were being cared for by too few nuns.

"A few weeks before you and your classmates were scheduled to leave St. Mary's, we began a campaign to get you ready for the move. We'd say things like, 'You better behave. When you're at SJH the brothers won't let you get away with mischief. They're tough, those brothers. Not like us.'

"We weren't totally unaware. We knew that you would be sad and afraid, and, I don't know if you remember, but a few sisters rode with you to St. John's Home in the small, twenty-five-seat purple van we owned. The driver was Mr. Flynn, a lay staff member who worked in the maintenance department as a groundskeeper.

"We expected tears. But when the van stopped in front of the new institution, every boy jumped off and headed away from us, without so much as a wave good-bye. We had hoped at least some of you would say good-bye."

I unpacked and went to lunch with my new dorm mates, who included some of the boys from St. Mary's as well as some other kids who had been transferred from other institutions.

Because I had done such a good job blocking out everything the sisters were trying to tell me, it came as a shock to discover that there were no sisters on the grounds. Not one. For the first time in my life, I was taking orders exclusively from a bunch of guys—the Order of Marianists. Instead of no-nonsense sisters, the brothers (as they were called), in conservative black suits with white dress shirts and black ties, were the ones waking me up in the morning and signaling lights out at night. I was plenty scared, and I began to get flashbacks of what Kevin had done. What was to keep one of the brothers from doing similar things? And I was homesick. I worried about Aunt Katherine. How was she going to find me? And if she did, would the brothers let her visit?

My New Home

My new dormitory looked like boot camp. It consisted of thirty-six twin metal frame beds, each with a spring and mattress. The beds were lined up in three rows of twelve going across the full width of the dormitory, with two feet between each bed and about three or four feet between each row. Each bed had a pillow, a gray, black-trimmed, institutional wool blanket, and a bedspread that was either green or brown. All the beds faced north, with windows on three sides all facing the Atlantic Ocean. The back two windows were directly above the ocean. Small, gray metal lockers with combination locks were placed between the windows on the north and south walls. Each boy had a locker assigned to him when he arrived. Only the front entrance and boardwalk separated us from the beach.

The plaster walls and window frames were painted standard institutional green and the floors were covered with standard twelve-inch brown tiles. The ceiling was white and the large floor radiators were silver. There were no curtains on the windows and no pictures on the walls. The overhead lighting consisted of three rows of eight-foot florescent lights that spread out over the entire length of the dorm. There were no table lamps.

The dormitory took up the width of the building, which was about forty feet wide and eighty feet long. Four identical dormitories were located on the second, third, and fourth floors of the institution. Upon entering the dormitory, to the right there was a small bathroom with light brown tiles. There were five sinks and toilets, four showers with shower curtains, and a large window so that the brother in charge could look in on us.

I was assigned to take a shower on three days each week. Bed linen was changed every Wednesday and I received my clean laundry back that day as well. All my personal clothes—my dungarees, socks, underwear, T-shirts, play shirts, and school plaid shirts—were marked with my assigned number. I was permitted in the dormitory only to sleep and when I had to change from my school clothes to play clothes at three o'clock. Otherwise, I was scheduled to spend most of my day in school, in the playground, or in the large recreation room on the first floor. There was no lounge area, there was no television. There was not even a radio.

But I had the ocean.

Learning a New Life

By the time I moved there, Rockaway Park and the surrounding area was like an aging diva. St. John's was situated in the middle of a community of summer bungalow rentals that, with their chipped rococo ornaments, could only hint at Rockaway's past glory as a summer haven for the rich. In season, the beach was swamped. I grew to love watching those vacationers—thousands of people lying out on the beach, making out, getting sun tans, and living their lives, oblivious to me. The brothers told me that Rockaway was where New Yorkers of very modest means went on vacation. But from my point of view, staring out the window of my crowded dormitory onto the beach, they looked like the richest folks in the world. I had never seen so many people in my life, and I fantasized that SJH was a vacation spot, not an institution.

The orphanage did not give us an allowance, so on weekends, while I was supposed to be swimming under the supervision of one of the brothers, I sneaked away and made some money collecting empty beer and soda bottles on the beach. I did not understand why guys who were making out with their girlfriends on blankets got nasty when I asked permission to take their empty bottles. I was always very polite; their responses were definitely less so.

"Beat it, kid."

"Take the damn bottles and get lost."

I cashed in the bottles at the White House Bar, which was enormous—it held a couple of hundred people, and during the summer that place really rocked. I was just eleven years old, and all I could do was watch in amazement. With my bottle money I bought junk food at St. John's canteen. St. Mary's never had the ocean and it never had a canteen. Chalk two up for SJH. And best of all, Aunt Katherine found me! She told me she had to take two subway trains and a bus, but she made it, and from then on we spent lovely summer afternoons walking on the boardwalk and going for lunch on Beach 116th Street, which was the main shopping area. She told me that Rockaway was the last stop on the subway from Brooklyn and Queens. But it all sounded foreign to me, as I had never been on a train or transit bus in my life.

Every Wednesday night in the summertime, SJH had a free band concert led by Brother Frank Springman, and people walking along the boardwalk came strolling in. Although the brothers passed the basket around, I could see that very few people contributed. The concert went from seven to nine and the band was pretty good. For a while I toyed with the idea of taking accordion or piano lessons in the music room. In fact, on Saturday or Sunday afternoons I spent hours practicing Beethoven's "Moonlight Sonata," which Brother Frank took pains to teach me. Even today, whenever I hear that sonata being played, I think fondly of SJH and Brother Frank. I wonder where life has taken him and what he is doing now.

Overall, Rockaway was a taste of paradise. My bed was next to the dorm window, from which I had a clear view of the Atlantic Ocean. I spent my free time staring out at the crashing waves, soothed and relaxed by the repetition. Daydreaming, I blocked out reality. I fantasized how I got to this place, where I was going, and what was in store for me. Whenever I felt depressed or down, I simply sat at the window of my dormitory and looked out at the sea.

Living next door to the Atlantic Ocean began to compensate for being trapped in yet another dreary institution, and little by little I forgot about the sisters.

Rockaway Playland

When I turned twelve, my world opened up when I was given permission to visit Rockaway Playland, a glorious amusement park on Beach 98th Street. No words can describe the joy that place gave me. There was the Atom Smasher, the Scenic Railroad, the Caterpillar Ride, the Switchblade Thriller, skee ball, and bumper cars. Even the entrance was thrilling—a huge grinning clown face that promised untold joys. Visiting Playland gave me a giddy sense of freedom. For a couple of hours at a time I was a child among children, a citizen in my own universe. To this day, I remember the aroma of popcorn and cotton candy mingling with the smell of ocean, boardwalk, and seaweed, and the sweet tinkle of the carousel. And candy apples! It was heaven. All a kid needed was the price of admission. Sometimes we went as a group with the dorm counselor. Other times, I was allowed to go by myself. Even if I didn't have money I could at least check it all out, and sometimes Aunt Katherine and I went there together. I loved the carousel, skee ball, and Ferris wheel, but I would only go on the roller coaster if my friends and I dared one another, and then we went together to show the world that we weren't punks.

Getting Out

In the winter, Rockaway became a ghost town. I made pocket money going door-to-door shoveling snow from people's driveways and walkways in Belle Harbor, a lovely neighborhood adjacent to St. John's. For the first time in my life, I met people who were not Catholic. They told me they were Jewish and were happy to give a boy from SJH a job so he would have money to buy candy and ice cream. They were really nice to me. I compared what I saw of their homes to where I lived and decided that these were rich people. I wanted to be rich and live like a rich person, but I did not have the foggiest notion of how to get there.

What I loved most about collecting empty bottles and shoveling people's driveways was that it got me out of the institution for a few hours. And I discovered pizza on Beach 116th Street, five blocks from the home. Even so, there were times I went nuts being stuck in the institution, day in and day out. So, although I knew I was a terrible basketball player, I joined SJH's Catholic Youth Organization (CYO) basketball team. Because we did not have an indoor basketball court, our home games were played at St. Francis de Sales, a Catholic parish in Belle Harbor around Beach 123rd Street. It was a very nice neighborhood. The houses were new, with manicured lawns and impeccably clean streets. They were nothing like the rundown homes and bungalows around SJH.

When we played other churches, Brother Frank Springman, our coach (he was also the music and band director), stopped on the way back to the home to buy the team soda and hot dogs at a place called the Big Bow Wow on Broad Channel Drive. Boy, was that great food! The hot dogs were grilled and the hamburgers charcoal broiled— what a change from the boiled hot dogs and oven-grilled hamburgers we got at St. John's. The Big Bow Wow made the best food I ever had in my life.

I joined the basketball team with my dorm mates, and it solidified my friendship with two excellent athletes, Jose Torado and Francisco Casiano, who were responsible for the team winning a lot of games. I was not nearly as athletic as either of them, but we were all good friends. Mostly they played while I sat on the sidelines. But even though I was a weak player, they appreciated that I hated losing. They discovered my competitive streak when we played softball and dodgeball in the SJH play yard when the weather permitted, and billiards and ping-pong when we had to stay indoors. (When we were not playing sports in summer, Jose, Francisco, Howard, Charlie, and I went swimming in the ocean every day. We were all pretty good swimmers.)

Organizations in Queens provided tickets for SJH boys and I went to Madison Square Garden for college basketball games and the circus, Radio City Music Hall for the Christmas show, and Yankee and Shea Stadium for both football and baseball games. I was still sitting in the rafters, and it was still tough going to all these events and watching people sitting next to me gorging themselves on delicious junk food, but what the heck! It was fun getting out of the institution, and once in a while a civic organization actually gave us money to buy snacks. Jose Torado and Francisco Casiano always went to sporting events, but other friends, like Charles Palagonia, Douglas Hampton, Howard Cienski, and Charlie Lynch, went only if they heard that we were getting food money.

Stage Struck

The Marianist Brothers introduced me to the world of tap dancing and singing groups. The nuns never gave me that! We had a professional tap dance instructor from the outside community to teach us his moves, and Brother Frank Springman took charge of the singing group. He also played the piano. In all my eleven years I had never met anybody as talented as him. He was a great person, and I added him to my list of men I wanted to be like when I grew up.

We SJH boys were so talented and well trained that we were invited to perform at the Brooklyn Academy of Music's school competition. Performing on stage in front of hundreds of people was the most exciting thing that had ever happened to me. Everyone loved us and it was a good lesson to discover that all our practice and hard work paid off. We received a standing ovation and, unbelievably, out of fifteen performance groups, St. John's Home was awarded first prize.

On the bus ride back, we were as excited as if we had won an Academy Award. Brother Frank sat behind the driver, quiet as a lamb, grinning from ear to ear for the entire trip.

Corporal Punishment

I remember Brothers Raymond Miclick, James Fitzgibbons, Charles Luttenberger, August Kemme, Charles Awalt, and, of course Brother Frank Springman. They all took good care of me. Corporal punishment was not the norm in St. John's Home. Generally, when a kid misbehaved the brothers would restrict him to the institution. Keeping a boy from going to the beach or to Rockaway Playland worked better than any corporal punishment they could have inflicted. Most of the brothers were cool even though they were strict, and by then most of us kids were already institutionalized and disciplined. Brothers would yell many threats to scare us, but, like the sisters, I found them to be more bark than bite. In fact, I recall only one brother, Brother Donald Gaskill, who actually spanked us when we misbehaved, and he did it more for show than to inflict pain. He was an excellent dormitory counselor and something of a nerd. In fact, most of the kids were a lot tougher than he was, but he compensated by carrying around a beautifully varnished mahogany spanking paddle that he had crafted himself in the institution-school wood shop. The paddle was so long that it accommodated three boys at a time. That paddle—it was a kind of joke we were all in on. We would misbehave and he would threaten to whack us one. We would ignore his threats and eventually, when he actually came through on his threat, we would scream and yell as though we were being killed. We were not, but it was part of the fun. Everyone knew it was for show.

The Ferocious Ocean

The ocean can terrify. Being a peninsula, Rockaway is so narrow that sometimes waves from one side can be seen merging with waves from the other side in a fearsome embrace.

One wintry night an ocean storm came up to the very steps of the building where I slept. Everyone lay trembling, waiting in terror for the Atlantic Ocean to come crashing through the window and drown us all. Would we be driven out to sea, hanging on to our beds for dear life? Was this really the end? It took the better part of the night for Brothers Raymond Miclick and Charles Littenburg to convince us that we were safe and that nobody would perish.

Altar Boy

With more than 140 boys at the institution, it was hard to get individual attention, but I was desperate to stand out from the others and get noticed in a special way. So sometime after my twelfth birthday I trained to become an altar boy. For months I studied one-on-one with the priest, learning Latin and training to perform all the duties and responsibilities that went with the job, such as bringing the priest water to wash his hands and ringing the bells at consecration. My favorite part was learning how to have a dialogue with the priest at the altar.

He would say, "In nomine Patris et Filii et Spiritus Sancti" (In the name of the Father, and of the Son, and of the Holy Spirit). My response: "Amen." Then he said, "Dominus Vobiscum" (The Lord be with you), to which I replied, "Et cum spiritu tuo" (And also with you). Finally, the priest said, "Agnus Dei, qui tollis peccata mundi, miserere nobis" (Lamb of God, you take away the sins of the world, have mercy on us), and I repeated it.

So, without telling anyone it was going to happen, one Sunday I appeared at the altar with the priest while he served Mass. My dorm mates were shocked, and afterward Jose and Francisco insisted on knowing where I learned all that Latin. They thought it was funny, mumbo jumbo stuff, but other kids, like Ernesto Martinez and Andy Velez, were impressed.

The priest tried to instill in me the importance of serving at the altar with humility, but it did not work. Every Sunday morning, as I made my way to the church in my black dress slacks, white shirt and dress shoes, my thoughts were not about God. All I could think of was that soon I would be standing up front at the altar and looking down at all the guys in the pews. It felt like I was the center of the universe, which was a very new feeling for me. The heady experience eventually translated into the grandiose conviction that I was as important as the priest at Mass. After all, Father was speaking to me in Latin, and I was answering him in that same mysterious language. I was pretty good at it, and I loved singing and praying in Latin as well. So what if I did not know what it all meant? Wasn't I up there, chatting with a priest in a language nobody else understood? I sometimes found myself imitating Father. I imagined I was a priest leading the Mass instead of just a kid in an altar boy getup.

I considered someday becoming a priest. It was very prestigious! I saw how respectfully the chaplain was treated at SJH, and I wanted to be treated the same way. But there was a part of me that knew it was a sham. I was not holy. I was just pretending. And as they say in the Bible, pride goes before a fall. If I had illusions of grandeur, the guys brought me down to earth with reality checks like, "Hey, Rohs, you think you're an angel or sumthin'? . . . I'll show you you're no angel, buddy," and "Wanna see an altar boy with a shiner? I'll show you one in a minute if you don't cut it out."

After a couple of years at St. John's, I began to trust the brothers and to forget Kevin. Brothers were in my life all the time. I relied on them the same way I had relied on Srs. Mary Aquinas, Mary Johanna,

Mary Joseph, and Mary Martha. I developed trust that they were good men—even holy men. I met a number of brothers from out of town who came to help out during summer and Christmas recess.

Nonetheless, there were times I secretly visited the chapel to pray. I would weep and ask God for forgiveness. I hid that side of me from the other kids; otherwise I would constantly get teased. I did not want anybody to think I was a "goody boy." But when things got tough at the institution, I found myself praying for support. I was only thirteen and confused about everything.

Betrayal

A visiting brother from Dayton, Ohio, goes out of his way to befriend me. I feel very fortunate to have Brother D. take a special interest in me and pay me so much attention. He lets me watch television in the quarters he shares with other brothers, but typically he invites me over when they are out supervising other kids or taking a break at the ocean. He gives me all kinds of snacks, and I feel like the luckiest kid in the world. I do not tell any of my dorm mates because I am afraid they might become jealous and take it out on me.

I convince myself that I have found a substitute for the father I never knew and that Brother D. is treating me like his son. I am proud that someone as prestigious as this man is taking a special interest in me, because, of course, like all the boys at the home, I am starved for affection. I am sorry to see him go when he leaves SJH and returns to his own institution in Ohio at the end of the summer. But, later that same year, he unexpectedly returns.

One night, while I am sound asleep in the dormitory, I feel someone's hand in my pajamas, playing with my private parts. I open my eyes and see Brother D., back for a visit. He is breathing hard as he tries to coax an erection from my paralyzed body. This is like a nightmare. I try to scream but nothing comes out. When he sees my shock, he disappears as suddenly as he arrived.

I do not see Brother D. again until the following summer, when once again he returns to SJH. And once again he comes around to my bed. But now I am a year older and determined to put a stop to his activities. I scream, "Get out of here," at the top of my lungs, hoping my cries will awaken the other boys and catch him in the act. No luck. I yell and Brother D. jumps from my bed and makes his escape.

It is the last time Brother D. bothers me. But I am an adolescent and the damage has been done. I feel my life is ruined. I am ashamed of myself for trusting this man, but I have no one in whom I can confide. I cannot tell the priest because I am afraid he will think I am lying and side with Brother D. And I cannot tell my friends because I know they will tease and call me names, and I will be in a fight every day. Now whenever Brother D. sees me he turns on his heels and goes in the opposite direction. In fact, the day after he tries to molest me, he receives Holy Communion at Sunday Mass in the chapel. I am astonished at his gall. How can he go up and receive the holy sacrament? Isn't he ashamed? I want to yell out in front of everyone in the chapel, "You bastard! How can you go up to take Communion after what you did to me?"

The sad part is that all the brothers who work year-round at SJH are really good and dedicated people. In fact, years later when I go back for a visit and tell the brothers about what happened, they are visibly shaken. They tell me that had they known, he would never have been allowed back. Perhaps I could have stopped him immediately. But how was a kid supposed to know what to do?

My hard-earned trust for men evaporates, and from that point on I keep my distance. I am on red alert and hypervigilant; I go into a shell and become withdrawn and guarded around male adults. Several of the other kids and brothers see a noticeable change in my behavior. They express concern but I am afraid of being teased so I keep my mouth shut. I am very confused and at a loss to deal with this trauma. I am sure that the only interest the brothers have in me is because they want to take advantage.

Prayer helps me deal with Brother D.'s abuse. If it were not for the comfort of prayer and the solitude of the chapel, I do not know how I ever would have gotten through this horrible time in my life. In time, the clear dedication and selflessness of the men who care for me day in, day out, exhibiting no ulterior motive, helps to heal the wound. Nevertheless, for as long as I live at SJH, I remain cautious of visiting brothers.

Staying Alive

Outside the institution, the community blamed the boys who lived at SJH for most of the local robberies and vandalism. Whenever there was a burglary in the nearby summer bungalows or houses, the police immediately came to SJH. Everyone thought we were juvenile delinquents and that the institution was a juvenile detention center. Whenever I walked around Rockaway Playland in my regulation poor kid clothes, I noticed that Playland employees eyed me suspiciously. I felt like I had St. John's Home for Boys written all over me.

Inside the institution the pecking order was ruthless, mirroring the rules of survival that are in play everywhere in the world: the strong bully the weak. At St. John's, the athletic boys bullied the nonathletic wimps. The kids who came to the institution from bad home situations were streetwise, and they lorded it over the kids who, like me, had lived their whole lives in institutional homes and did not know about street gangs and drugs. So where did I fit in? My eyeglasses were thicker than the bottom of a soda bottle, which, in theory, put me in the category of "victim," a kid who was ripe for bullying. New arrivals to the home thought I was a pushover, which was a mistake. Although I was not the kind of kid who started fights, I would never back down either. Someone just had to push the wrong button. I could take a lot teasing, but I was proud that Ed Rohs, a four-eyed, goofy-looking kid, was tough. Everyone knew

I could be pushed just so far before I would fight back. In fact, it was great to hear the kids say, "Ed Rohs may look goofy but he's no punk."

On the other hand, being nearly blind made me a total dud on the playing field and a prime target for teasing. I prayed for rain whenever my dorm was scheduled to play softball, but those prayers seemed never to be answered. When I played outfield, I would send up a fervent prayer that nobody hit the ball to me, but of course they did, because they knew my ineptitude would help their team score.

So I could not have been happier when the home decided it was time to send me to the Brooklyn Eye and Ear Hospital for a proper eye examination. Not only did I look forward to getting away for a couple of hours, but I hoped that maybe—just maybe—the doctors could improve my vision so I would finally stop hearing players on the opposing team yell, "Hit the ball to Eddie Rohs, he can't see the ball, he's blind as a bat." Worse than hearing this was knowing that the players would listen and try to hit every ball in my direction. But what really pissed me off was that I couldn't blame them. (Of course, the brothers told me to turn the other cheek. "Sticks and stones can hurt your bones but names can never harm you" or some other malarkey. I politely nodded my head, but underneath my breath, I was saying, "Bulls--t.")

One fine day we drive all the way from Rockaway Park to the Brooklyn Eye and Ear Hospital, but instead of perking me up, the trip is downright depressing. The hospital walls are painted institutional green, the chairs are hard, and the unflattering fluorescent glare gives everyone a yellow cast. The longer we wait for the doctor the worse it becomes. I do not like the feel of the place, and so finally I ask my escort from the home, "How come I can't go to a private doctor in Rockaway Park?" And this is when I get an important lesson in where I stand in the larger social pecking order. She tells me that the home does not have the money to pay for a private doctor and that the public clinic is where poor people in the community go when they need medical care. I look around and notice that everyone except my escort and me are black and Hispanic—just like the guys at the home. A light goes on in my brain: being in an orphanage means I am poor, and the other guys are poor, too.

I return to the hospital several times but they do not seem able to help. Finally, somebody at the home decides that maybe I should be sent to a private doctor. They make an appointment for me to see Dr. Naples, who has a practice right on Beach 116th Street, five blocks from the home. I walk into his private office and take a seat, but am I too excited to sit still. For the first time in my life I feel like a rich kid. The reception area is decorated beautifully. There are magazines to read. The walls are pastel and there is carpeting on the floor. The staff treats me like a valuable human being and not just a number. There are just a few patients and they speak to one another in hushed voices. It is quiet and peaceful, a world of difference from the noisy public clinic. I am on cloud nine, and after I see Dr. Naples I decide I want to be an eye doctor in a crisp white coat, healing poor people and being adored. When the home tries to convince me to return to the hospital for subsequent visits, I find a thousand excuses

A Sweet Brooklyn Memory

Sometimes I sneak away from the home to ride the A train back and forth from Rockaway Park into Brooklyn. I am fourteen and the brothers think I am at Playland. I figure that if they do not know where I am going they cannot stop me from going there. So I lie.

I plant myself in the first car so I can look out of the grimy front window as the train zooms past local stations at what feels to me like a hundred miles an hour. Passengers come and go but I stay at my window, transfixed by the moving stations, the play of shadow and light, and the exhilaration of shooting through the tunnel with no destination.

to not go. I have been shown how a person should be treated and I never want to go back to being a charity case.

Aunt Katherine's Mansion

Aunt Katherine was my mainstay. She visited me, and every year on my birthday fancy cookies would arrive in elegant Abraham & Straus department store boxes. There were birthday cards, too, but now that I was older they came with money tucked inside. Oh, how I looked forward to those birthday cards! During the summer months, Aunt Katherine came to see me on Sundays. We strolled along the boardwalk and she treated me to lunch on Beach 116th Street at a coffee shop that no longer exists. I did not realize how lucky I was to have her.

Ever since we first met I fantasized about my Aunt Katherine's wealth and her opulent lifestyle, and the first time I was given permission by SJH to travel by train to her house by myself I was excited beyond words. Finally, I would get to see the mansion! One Saturday I took the subway to Sunset Park, Brooklyn. There I discovered that Katherine McCarthy—my "Aunt" Katherine, who carried herself with such grace and dignity—lived in a row house in a working-class neighborhood.

I was shocked and sorely disappointed. There would be no limousines, and no magic solutions to the problems of my miserable life. She would never adopt me and take me away. How could she do this to me? I was really stuck. And yet she remained my Aunt Katherine and she still filled my life. I was always proud to be with her. And no matter where she lived, Katherine was still the quintessential 1950s lady, dressing impeccably, always touching up her red lipstick, powdering her nose, or lighting a Marlboro cigarette. My Aunt Katherine had a weekly appointment at the beauty parlor—wow! Sometimes when I visited she came to the door wearing a housedress, but she always changed into a nice outfit before going into public. In fact,

I do not remember ever seeing my Aunt Katherine unkempt, and although she hated the fuss of the kitchen, sometimes she would break down and create a great meal for me. And unlike meals at the orphanage, there were always seconds.

Katherine shared her Irish heritage with me, and I, being totally ignorant of my own family, eagerly adopted it for myself. We sometimes listened to Irish songs on WFUV, the Fordham University radio station. It was such sad music, and I loved it because the words and melodies resonated so strongly with my state of mind. Her favorite song was "Four Green Fields." She told me the history of Ireland and how proud she was to be a member of the Order of Hibernians. I was quite surprised when, years later, I discovered that I was of German stock. I somehow assumed that I was Irish, like Sr. Johanna and Aunt Katherine.

Role Models

With the exception of Sunday afternoon professional football games—the Cleveland Browns with Jim Brown is my favorite team—weekends are a crashing bore. To pass the time I play billiards and ping-pong in the recreation room or take long walks on the boardwalk. After school the kids at SJH can use their allowance to buy candy, soda, potato chips, and ice cream. But Sunday is the one day of the week when we all get treated to candy and a soda. Our benefactor is a nice old man—"Pops"—who donates the money for these treats. I met Pops once and thought he was the nicest person in the world. After our meeting I decide that when I grow up I will be a kind gentleman. Kids will love me. Maybe they will call *me* Pops, too.

Two other people who donate to SJH also make weekend visits. A distinguished-looking man sometimes drives up in a beautiful Lincoln Continental. I love his car and I know it is expensive. I ask the director what the car owner does for a living, and I find out that the gentleman, John Lynch, is a senior vice president of the Kings County Trust Company in downtown Brooklyn. Then and there I decide I will be a senior vice president of a bank, and for a start I make it my business to observe how he carries himself. I tell myself that when I grow up I, too, will buy a Lincoln Continental. Another man who volunteers his weekends to spend time with us at St. John's is a lieutenant in the New York City Police Department. His name is Patrick Fitzsimmons, and being a cop, all the kids think he is really cool. I hope to someday become a NYC police officer just like him.

So, at fourteen, I dream of becoming a banker, a philanthropist, or a police lieutenant, I do not much care which. I have already concluded that I do not have the moral fiber to be a man of the cloth. I like the attention and the benefits, but I have to admit that I do not think Our Lord would appreciate my desire for the limelight. (And I have decided against becoming a doctor—All that schoolwork! All that blood!) Every weekend I check to see if either the banker or the police lieutenant have come to visit. When the lieutenant visits, I tell him I am going to grow up and be just like him, and he encourages me in my fantasy. Why not? There will be time enough for me to find out that with my poor vision there is no chance that I will be accepted to the force.

Sometimes I wonder what my father did for a living before he died. I wonder how he died. And my mother? Had they been in an accident? In my personal creation myth, I imagine that I was born to beautiful people—like Mr. Lynch and Pops—who took their shiny Lincoln Continental out for a ride and were killed in an awful accident, which explains how I ended up in an orphanage. Maybe they were spies working for the president and were killed by the communists. I did not understand why no one ever showed up to claim me. Could it be that nobody knew where I was? There was no way I could find out what happened for sure because nobody at the institution said a word. It was a secret.

Then one day, out of nowhere, my social worker, Elena Curella, calls me into her office and tells me that my parents are alive and that she is trying to locate them. Ms. Curella is a very young, very idealistic, and in many ways a very naive caseworker who believes she is making a discovery that will change my life. In a way, she is right.

Mom and Dad

I am in complete shock. My parents are alive and we will be reunited. I keep all my appointments with Ms. Curella, and every time she reports back to me that she is making progress I became more excited until, too late, she realizes that she has made a big mistake. I tell her I am sure they are rich and live in a mansion in the suburbs, and she tries to bring me down to earth, but by then I am too far gone. I am already daydreaming about reconciliation and planning for the day when I will leave the orphanage forever. I cannot concentrate in school. I cannot sleep at night. Then, for months I hear nothing from Ms. Curella, which drives me crazy but also gives me free rein to embellish my ever more lavish dreams. (One house? Why not two?)

Finally Ms. Curella sends me a message to come to her office. She has spoken with my parents. I wriggle with excitement. What do they look like? Where do they live? How soon do they want to see me? When can I visit? Why did they put me in the orphanage? Do I have any brothers or sisters? What does my father do for a living? She cannot keep up with all the questions, and in my excitement I grab her and give her a big hug. I am out of control. But as soon as she begins her story, I realize that the news is not good. She describes their tenement home in detail. My parents are very poor people. It is not anything I expected. I am almost fourteen and I have jumped to all kinds of conclusions without knowing the real story. For the first time in my life, I hear who my parents are and where I come from.

I cannot begin to describe how excruciatingly painful it is to sit in that social worker's office and listen to what she is saying. She explains that my parents are struggling to make ends meet. They never married, but they are caring for my brother and sister, twins who were born in 1955. In a nutshell, their lives border on destitution. And without spelling it out, she makes it clear that they do not want anything to do with me. But the good news, she tells me, is that after much coaxing she has convinced them to send me a birthday card. Outraged, I scream, "I don't give a s--t about a card!"

Weeks later I apologize for my outburst. She is very kind and understanding. When the birthday card arrives in the mail, I am excited and angry at the same time. I rush over to Ms. Curella's office to show it to her. It is a cheap, tacky card—nothing like the lovely cards I receive from Aunt Katherine. And it is signed simply "Mom and Dad." The handwriting is childlike. I am overwhelmed with complicated feelings and I need Ms. Curella to help me sort them out right then but she cannot see me immediately. It is the final straw. I stand outside her office and rip the card up in a million little pieces—the first and only birthday card I ever receive from my parents.

Elena Curella never gets to see the card, which is the result of her hard work, and we never talk about my parents again.

Brother August

Brother August is the director of St. John's Home for Boys. He is a heavyset man with broad shoulders, someone careless of his physical appearance who comes across as tough as nails. But under his gruff exterior he is an administrator of great compassion and determination. When Brother August finds out I am failing all my classes, he is shocked. I was a top student at St. John's and now suddenly, in my last year, I am in danger of being left back. He has no idea that the guys who come back to visit after graduating to St. Vincent's love to tell us eighth graders horror stories about how we are about to spend the next four years of our lives hiding from drug dealers and dodging bullets from gangs lurking just outside the institution's gates. I am honestly terrified, but there is no one I can talk to about it. So to

Graduation from St. John's Home for Boys. I'm top row left.

save my life I cook up a plan to flunk out of eighth grade and be held back a year.

Brother August calls me into his office and tries to discover what is happening to me; he speaks to my social worker; he chats informally with me when we meet in the halls.

"How's everything going, Ed?"

"Good, Brother August. Everything's going good."

Of course, in retrospect, my decision to be left back intentionally is very shortsighted and results in some serious consequences. Because I fail my classes in eighth grade, I am transferred out of my advanced classes and placed with slower boys. Worse, when I finally graduate and go on to high school, school guidance counselors register me for classes that lead to a "general diploma" rather than an "academic diploma." In other words, I am not placed in programs designed to move me along a track leading to college. It takes years for me to clean up the negative consequences of a decision I made when I was thirteen.

Sometime before leaving St. John's, I am taken down to the social worker's office and told I have to choose a high school. All of a sudden, literally overnight, I have to decide whether I want to go to Erasmus Hall or John Jay, both in Brooklyn. Perhaps I want to attend a school in Manhattan? If so, there is Washington Irving or Chelsea Vocational. And there are more—lots more. Because I am coming from an institution, there are no zoning restrictions. I can go anywhere I want. I think about it, and it turns out that "anywhere I want" is anywhere there are girls.

I choose to attend John Jay High School because some friends a year ahead have told me it is an OK place, and because some of my buddies will be going there as well. But mostly I go because, for the first time in my life, I will get to sit in a classroom with girls.

8 St. Vincent's Home for Boys

66 Boerum Place
Brooklyn, New York

A Brief History: The Newsboys' Home

On December 8, 1858, the evening of the Feast of the Immaculate Conception, in a gas-lit classroom at St. James School in Brooklyn, Bishop John Loughlin exhorted members of the Brooklyn St. Vincent de Paul Society to find ways to alleviate the suffering of indigent newsboys. The men in that room were far from rich, but they were well respected in the community and committed to helping the underclass. And Bishop Loughlin had already proved himself an ardent and powerful proponent of building services to promote the well-being of the most vulnerable in his diocese.

Seven years later, at another meeting of the same group, Reverend Francis J. Freel proposed "to provide shelter for homeless boys who slept out of doors, and lived from hand to mouth without benefit of education or religion." Bernard Bogan, president of the society, further amplified the proposal by suggesting they provide "a real home, where boys would find security, comfort and protection."

What these men accomplished was astonishing. Painstakingly they raised the requisite $5,500 for the down payment on a house, plus the additional money required for alterations and repairs. Ten years after Bishop Loughlin first brought the issue to the top of the

The *Brooklyn Eagle*: Christmas 1880

Each inmate of St. Vincent's Home for Boys received on Christmas Eve an article of clothing, including flannel shirts, jackets, pantaloons, or socks—all of the best material.

The services on Christmas Day began with early Mass, and breakfast with meat followed. During the day the boys found some of the graduates of the home or received visits from them. A lunch with cake and fruit was served at noon.

Sixty boys sat down to the dinner, which consisted of roast turkey and cranberry sauce, roast beef, vegetables, bread, plum pudding, fruits, and sweetmeats. The evening was spent in the gymnasium, where they amused themselves by singing and playing theater, telling anecdotes, and dealing charades.

The Christmas contributions were from Miss M. A. McSorley, of Bridge Street, $10; Mrs. James Johnson of Quincy Street, $10; Mr. James McMahon, of McDougal Street, two turkeys; Mr. J. F. Becker, of Front Street, table raisins; Mr. Charles S. Higgins, of 6th Avenue, three turkeys; Mr. M. Baker of Fulton Market, twenty pounds of beef.

agenda, the men of the Society of St. Vincent had collected enough money to proceed with their plan. For $14,000 the society purchased a home at 7 Poplar Street, near the old Eagle Building in downtown Brooklyn. And on July 19, 1869, they obtained the certificate of incorporation for the "Saint Vincent's Home of the City of Brooklyn for the Care and Instruction of Poor and Friendless Boys, who were by necessity compelled to engage in and pursue some industrial occupation . . . that the further object and business was to rescue said boys from evil associations—to qualify them to discharge the duties of useful and respectable citizens as well as to enable them in future life to earn an honest and honorable livelihood."

This home was unique. It was not designed to be an orphanage, but rather a shelter "to rescue boys from evil associations, to help them become respectable citizens and earn an honest living."

And so they came, newsboys as young as seven and as old as sixteen. It was close to the Fulton Ferry, and convenient for boys who lived on the streets near the Brooklyn docks. They could pick up their daily load at newspaper plants and run to the foot of the ferry, where they sold their papers to arriving passengers.

The official name was St. Vincent's Home of the City of Brooklyn for the Care and Instruction of Poor and Friendless Boys, but after awhile, for the sake of brevity and in keeping with the temporary residents who passed through its doors, the name was shortened to the Newsboys Home. A year after its opening, the St. Vincent de Paul Society of New York established a similar home at 53 Warren Street in New York. The ambitious aim of that home was nothing less than the "feeding, clothing, and sheltering the destitute children of the huge Empire City by the sea, and also [to] educate them in book-learning, strengthen industrious habits, inculcate self-respect and self-reliance, all grounded on a solid religious education, and thus infuse an ambition into them of becoming something more noble and more useful than newsboys and bootblacks."

Boys in both locations paid five cents for a meal and five cents for lodging. The Brooklyn home had a gym, which was outfitted on one side with a stage for dramatic presentations. The dorms were warm and clean, and the food far better than that of many poor families of New York. Five nights a week the boys were taught to read and write. In 1906 the Brooklyn home moved to its present location at 66 Boerum Place on the corner of State Street. It was a state-of-the-art facility, with a roof garden, a playground, recreation rooms, and a bowling alley. The St. Vincent's Home for Boys now could accommodate more than two hundred boys.

It was a huge improvement over the dreadful conditions that existed before the creation of the two newsboys homes. By the time

At age fifteen I was transferred to St. Vincent's Home. I lived here until I graduated from high school.

I arrived at St. Vincent's in 1961, the newsboys and their historic strike were the stuff of legend. The bowling alley and roof garden were long gone, and the state-of-the-art building was crumbling.

Reprieve

If Rockaway was a poor man's paradise, downtown Brooklyn in 1961 was hell. I was fifteen years old when I left St. John's and went to live in St. Vincent's Home for Boys. What can I say about St. Vincent's? Well, it was on the border between elegant Brooklyn Heights and a drug-infested slum, and adjacent to the county jail and courthouses. I was terrified that I would be mugged, beaten up, sexually violated. Adding to the mix, I had a clear sense that the moment I walked through those doors—bam—my childhood was over. St. Vincent's was the last stop before I was legally emancipated and no longer a ward of the state. When I graduated from high school, ready or not, I would have to leave the only world I had ever known and fend for myself outside the confines of institutional life. Right after graduation in June, a bus picked us up at SJH and delivered us to Boerum Place. We stepped onto the Brooklyn pavement like condemned men awaiting their fate.

And then a miracle happened! Before I even got a chance to look around, we were all herded into another bus and driven away—to Camp Christopher, a ten-week sleepaway summer camp for St. Vincent's boys in Columbia, New Jersey, near the Delaware Water Gap. Camp Christopher was beautiful and I immediately fell in love with the place. Each cabin had five bunk beds with only ten campers in each cabin. I was used to living with up to seventy kids in a dormitory with one counselor, and now there were three counselors in each cabin. Was it possible that this paradise belonged to St. Vincent's Home?

Later, I was told that Monsignor Casey and the board of directors of St. Vincent's established the camp in 1954. The upkeep and operation of the camp were funded entirely by donations. To raise money for the property and to build the actual camp, St. Vincent's initially held a fund-raising dinner, which then became an annual event at the St. George Hotel in Brooklyn Heights. St. Vincent's staff and dormitory counselors were required to work at the camp all summer long, but the social workers took turns.

Camp was all fun and games. There was arts and crafts, canoeing, swimming, hiking, volleyball, basketball, and softball. You name it and Camp Christopher's had it. The place was run by a former St. Vincent's boy, John McGinley, a tough little man of many talents. John had a black belt in judo, which was a useful skill to have if you were camp director for a bunch of angry adolescent boys; he was also the St. Vincent's organist and director of the dormitory counselors at the home.

It was a glorious introduction to my new home, but eventually summer ended, and on a sun-drenched September morning the camp closed and we were back on the bus going to St. Vincent's.

Leaving Camp Christopher.

We had used up our miracle and this time we were going to Boerum Place for real. What a depressed bunch of kids we were on the ride back to the city—too sad to even speak or mess around. As the bus hurtled along the highway, taking us to meet our fate, a childcare supervisor read off each boy's dorm assignment, and some of the guys who were a year ahead and knew the ropes advised the newcomers where to go when we arrived.

I step off the bus with my small bag of worldly possessions packed in a regulation black plastic garbage bag and walk up the cement steps into the creepy, decrepit tan brick building that houses 145 angry, testosterone-laden adolescent boys. Straightaway, some guy orders me to my dorm on the third floor and, butterflies fluttering in my gut, I walk down the dingy hallway that leads to the central stairway, which in turn leads to the dormitories. A group of the toughest guys I have ever seen—white, black, and Hispanic—hoot and scream "New Vinnie Boys!" as they size up the newcomers and work with great success to scare me half out of my wits. But no matter what I am feeling, I know enough to keep walking and above all to avoid eye contact. After spending my life in institutions, I know that all it takes is for one guy to turn me into a mark by uttering the dreaded words: "Who the hell you lookin' at?" But as I move along the corridor—left foot in front of right in front of left—*God, please get me out of here*—a couple of kids from St. John's recognize me and shout, "Hey, Eddie, how ya doin'?" They give me a high five, which is code for *Ed Rohs is one of us. He's not a punk, he's cool.* Still I keep face forward and continue walking. I know my tormentors will never stop looking for a chink in my armor, and when they find it, God help me if I don't have powerful allies on my side. In fact, the older kids at camp have already warned me, "Don't act like a punk." Walking down that hall, with the jeers and stares and catcalls, I do everything in my power to follow their advice.

When I reach my dormitory, I am introduced to Mr. Ralph Kelly. (I already knew from camp that all staff are addressed as "Mister." I am never to call anyone by his first name.) I catch a glimpse of gritty windows that open onto an inner-city urban landscape, with vistas of the Brooklyn House of Detention on one side and congested Atlantic Avenue on the other. Mr. Kelly assigns me a bed, a folding metal chair, and a locker, and he hands me a combination Master lock.

"We're not responsible for anything stolen from your locker. Keep that in mind."

OK, Mr. Kelly, thank you, Mr. Kelly. I will, Mr. Kelly. At St. John's Home it was always, "Yes, brother," "No, brother," and "Thank you, brother." And at St. Mary of the Angels Home it was always "Yes, Sister." At St. Vincent's Home for Boys it is "Yes, Mr. Kelly."

Ralph Kelly is African American, and he is the first dorm counselor I ever had who was not a member of a religious order. He is not even Catholic. At St. Vincent's most of the staff were lay employees, with the exception of Monsignor Casey, who ran the place, and the four nuns who worked in the kitchen, laundry room, and infirmary. Mr. Kelly is the complete opposite of what I have been told to expect of a dormitory counselor. He is a big man—over six feet tall and about 260 pounds. But he is cool, calm, and well mannered, and he definitely does not fit the stereotype of a sadistic dorm counselor who beats kids up. I immediately take a liking to him.

At every institution I have been to, upon arrival I get a new set of clothing with a laundry number. Mr. Kelly sends me to the second floor, where I meet Sister Mary Henrietta, a tough-as-nails German nun who runs the laundry room like her own private empire. She distributes all the clothes, bed linens, washcloths, and towels on Wednesdays after school, and any item she issues is accounted for in a notebook she keeps on the counter. Sr. Mary Henrietta is totally fearless. She rules over us like a tyrant, and it does not take long for me to realize that her bite is every bit as bad as her bark. At Christmas Sr. Henrietta wraps our clean laundry in red-and-green holiday paper. Merry Christmas!

But on my first day all she does is recite in a monotone (with a thick German accent that I have a hard time understanding) all the rules and regulations pertaining to laundry. I cannot believe laundry could be so complicated, but I energetically nod in agreement. The bottom line is simple—if you do not turn in your dirty laundry you do not get your clean laundry back. She loads me down with my weekly allotment of towels, sweat socks, Fruit of the Loom underwear and T-shirts, pajamas, dungarees, polo shirts, plus toothpaste, a toothbrush, and a bar of Ivory soap. I also get a new pair of standard black-and-white Converse sneakers and a bathrobe. Someone has written the number 161 with a laundry-marking pen on everything. For the next four years that number will identify everything I own.

I return to my space in the dorm, arrange my stuff in the half-length locker, lock it with my new Master combination lock, and then race down the main stairwell, through the basement, and out to a fenced-in yard. I sit down on the concrete floor with my back propped up against a brick wall. Traffic noise and the deafening shriek of police and fire sirens overwhelm my senses. In all my life I have never seen so many cars and buses in one place at the same time. Up until now I have lived in quiet residential institutions where the loudest noise was the whirr of a car making its way up the suburban street—and, of course, the ocean.

My eyes turn to Atlantic Avenue. Mr. Kelly has already warned me that it is off-limits.

"If you go to Atlantic Avenue you're taking your life into your hands. The same goes for Smith and Pacific Streets. Don't forget. That's where addicts are dealing drugs and gangs hang out."

The one exception, I am told, is Pop's candy store, right across the street. Pop's is where everyone got their candy and soda and single cigarettes for a nickel apiece.

From the Atlantic Ocean to Atlantic Avenue. I lean against the brown wall and think helplessly of my future in this noisy, over-crowded, six-story slum. How can there be drug dealers right across the street from the jail and the courthouse, with all the cops and judges and lawyers? Isn't anyone in charge? Am I going to end up getting locked up, too? How am I going to survive?

But there is nothing I can do. I know I am going to have to live like this until I graduate from high school, which feels like light-years away. It is a hot and muggy day and I am terribly homesick for St. John's. I idly wonder how it can be that the same people who run Camp Christopher also run St. Vincent's. Who are these people? How could the Church let this happen to me?

A Tour of My New Home

After a while I pull myself together, get up off the ground, and go to explore my new home. The first place I go is the basement be-cause it is where the kitchen and dining rooms are located. It also houses the main shower room and athletic locker room, as well as some other stuff, like the maintenance and the boiler rooms. On the first floor there is a recreation room, social worker, switchboard operator/public address announcer, and chapel. The administrative offices, auditorium, and laundry room are all on the second floor. Most important, it has the rectory. This is where Monsignor Casey, who heads the place, has his office, and it is also where he lives. The older boys have already let me know that his apartment drives them crazy. Why? The gist of their argument is that he lives like a king on the second floor while on the third and fourth floors the boys live in a slum. I'm dying to see what it looks like, but there is no way I'm going to barge into the monsignor's office, and there isn't a chance I'll get to enter his private living quarters.

The third and fourth floors each have three dormitories and one bathroom, and each bathroom has only two showers. The fifth floor is multipurpose—there is a small gymnasium, an infirmary, and a convent for the four nuns who do the housework. Finally, on the sixth floor I discover a small dormitory for twelve of the oldest boys, along with an enclosed roof that is off-limits to everybody. Adjacent to the building I find our play yard and an asphalt football practice yard, as well as a garage and a small boxing gym.

The biggest shocker about St. Vincent's Home, as I've said, is that I am no longer being cared for by people from a religious order. Aside from the monsignor and the four nuns, the institution is run by secular men—from the administrator, Robert Fitzpatrick, and the director of social work, Louis Menachino, to John McGinley, director of dormitory counselors and camp director. In no way does it feel like a religious institution, except on Sundays when we have to attend Mass in the chapel.

Toeing the Line

My schedule is strict and followed with militaristic precision. Following is a typical school day.

6:00 A.M.	Reveille
6:30	Breakfast for older boys

7:00	Breakfast for younger boys
7:30	Dining room is closed
8:00	All dormitories are closed and I go to school
3:00 P.M.	I return from school. Dormitory counselors come back on duty and dorms are opened.
3:00–5:00	Free time (recreation room and play yard open)
5:00	Dinner for younger boys
5:30	Dinner for older boys
6:00–7:00	Free time (recreation room and play yard open)
7:00–9:00	Study hall
9:00–10:00	Shower time. Get ready for bed. Snacks are distributed.
10:00	Bedtime. Lights out in all dormitories.

The Public Address System

My life at St. Vincent's is dominated by the public address system. It blares orders from wake-up to the final call of the day: "All lights out, it's bedtime."

Speakers are everywhere—in each of the six dorms and the playground. They are mounted high on the wall of both the first-floor recreation room and the second-floor auditorium. Speakers are in all the hallways, the dining room, and the kitchen. No kid can use the excuse that he did not hear his name being called; no one can say he missed the wake-up call, meal call, study hall call, or bedtime announcement. In fact, if you are anywhere in the building you would not be able to go anywhere without hearing some kind of announcement. When we try to watch a movie in the auditorium or television in the dormitory, there is always at least one exasperated kid who would yell, "Shut that f----g thing off!"

The only places that do not have speakers are the chapel, the bathrooms, the dormitory counselors' bedrooms, the infirmary, and the rectory. The switchboard operator in charge of the public address system begins the day's torture at six in the morning by blasting reveille and announcing, "Wake-up call, rise and shine, wake-up call, rise and shine," followed immediately by soft classical music from the Paterson, New Jersey, radio station WPAT. With slight variations, every boy has the same thought: "What's this crap they're playing?" I know because some of us don't keep these thoughts to ourselves.

And as the gentle music plays, staff members handle a late riser by flipping the mattress and hurling him to the floor. Once, right after my arrival at St. Vincent's, I got thrown to the floor, hitting my head so hard I thought I had a concussion. It was the last time I tried sleeping in. Some dormitory counselors bring cups of cold water to encourage us to "rise and shine." Whoever had the idea of playing music to chill us out did not know Vinnie Boys. On any given morning, while the PA system croons sweetly, some kid who has been doused with cold water may try to start a riot.

"Hit him, hit him!"

Other kids just curse out the counselor, and the following Saturday they get to curse some more after their allowance is whittled down as punishment.

The music plays on while we make our beds, get out of our pajamas, and put on our school clothes. Sometimes the childcare director, John McGinley, interrupts the sappy music to make a special announcement. At six thirty there is another announcement: "Dorms One and Two report to the dining room for breakfast."

The boys race down to the basement, followed by their dorm counselors. We have fifteen minutes for breakfast, but a burly staff member assigned to guard the door stops us from running past him until the dorm counselor arrives to supervise us so that we eat in our assigned area. At six forty-five the ritual is repeated: "Dorms Three and Four, report to the dining room for breakfast." And finally, at seven thirty: "Last call for breakfast, last call for breakfast."

Stragglers run down and try to get into the dining room. This can be a very anxious time for the counselor on duty, and he and the dorm counselor have to decide whether to believe the boy's reason for not making it to his meal with his dorm mates.

After breakfast, which I eat at breakneck speed, I run back upstairs to my dormitory to finish my chores and get my schoolbooks and subway tokens for the journey to John Jay High School and the return trip back to the home.

At eight o'clock the music stops and the speaker blasts a warning notice: "All dormitories close in fifteen minutes. All dormitories close in fifteen minutes."

People walking or driving to work on Atlantic Avenue and Boerum Place can hear the announcements and orders being blasted loud and clear, making it clear to one and all that the brick building on the corner was an institution for boys.

After we leave for school, the speaker continues to blare messages for boys who are legally still in the building: "Ed Rohs, report to the infirmary," or "Ed Rohs, report to your social worker on the first floor."

If I am sick, I have the option of going up to the infirmary to see the nurse, who won't ever let anybody stay there unless they are near death. She is actually a lot like Nurse Ratched in *One Flew Over the Cuckoo's Nest.* If there is a formal reason why I cannot go to class—if I have a doctor's appointment or the social worker needs to see me, or if I feel too sick to go to school—I am usually sent to sit in the second-floor auditorium. Nothing is provided to cut the tedium. In fact, for a teenage boy it may be the most boring place on earth. (Face it, if the auditorium were fun, you would have kids lining up to get in with every excuse in the book.) A counselor is assigned to auditorium duty to make sure no one tries to escape, because the dormitories are locked until three o'clock.

When the dorm opens at three, the switchboard operator recites what is open, what is happening, what we have to do. Repeatedly we hear about all the wonderful options available. If the speakers were not placed so high and out of reach, I have no doubt that we would be throwing our Converse sneakers at the damn things to shut them up.

Some announcements cause a mad rush—mealtime is one. Another is "Dorm Three, pick up your clean sheets. The laundry room is

A typical dorm room in St. Vincent's in the 1960s.

closing in five minutes." Sister Henrietta has no problem closing the laundry room door in our face if it is past closing time.

And at four forty-five the PA system informs us, "All recreation areas are closed. All recreation areas are closed. All residents report to your dormitories and prepare for supper, all residents report to your dormitories and prepare for supper." Then, in a repeat of the morning ritual, "Dorm One report to the dining room for supper . . ."

On and on until the final announcement of the day: "All lights out, all lights out, last call, all lights out."

Amen.

Mealtime at St. Vincent's

At a quarter past five in the evening, the public address system would announce that my dormitory had to report to the dining room for supper. A burly dorm counselor was assigned to the dining room entrance to make sure kids did not sneak in before their dormitory was called over the PA system. Every night he got hassled by some kid trying to sneak in ahead of time or cutting the line. Keeping order was quite a job, and he got ticked off when dorm counselors didn't help him out by coming down with their group when their dorm was called.

The dining room took its cue from the military. Meals were served on metal trays, cafeteria-style. Food was thrown on my plate like it was swill, which actually is a pretty accurate description of what the stuff looked and tasted like. The food at St. Vincent's was awful, especially in comparison to St. John's and St. Mary's. It looked bad and tasted worse. But I got used to it—otherwise I would have starved. In fact, it is amazing that, in time, I actually talked myself into developing a taste for the stuff.

Every morning an Ebinger's pastry truck dropped off big metal trays piled high with day-old pastries. We were constantly being reminded how lucky we were to have one of the best bakeries in the city send us pastries every day. Unfortunately, the home did not provide staff to supervise the distribution of these goodies, or even serving utensils so we could pick them up one at a time. It was really disgusting, because we had to paw our way through piles of glazed prune, cheese, cinnamon, and pecan danish until they turned into a mess of gouged and gummy trash. Still, I dove in like everybody else because after I finished eating the breakfast that had just been served—the boiled egg, cold toast, and corn flakes or hot cereal—I was still hungry. To this day, I wonder what Mr. and Mrs. Ebinger would have said if they knew that their pastry was being served like food to cattle, rather than with respect on individual cake dishes.

Sometimes there were food fights and explosive arguments in the dining room. Most times it was between the guys, but there were times when it was directed at the kitchen help, Mr. and Mrs. Horn, who were really nice people. They got the brunt of our frustration because they were on the front lines, serving this slop to us. The cook also served the hot food. He was a fat slob who wiped the sweat that poured off his face with a grimy apron as he doled out our meals. He got even more of the abuse than Mr. and Mrs. Horn, because he did not care how he looked or how he presented the food. The message he sent us was that he didn't give a damn about us.

I usually did not complain, because from a young age the sisters had drilled into me the idea that I was fortunate to have a roof over my head and three meals a day. The one time I complained, my dorm counselor snapped back, "There's the door and don't let it hit you on the way out."

Vinnie Boys

At SJH our nickname was "Jack's Boys," and at St. Vincent's Home we were "Vinnie Boys." Whether I was out in the community or at school, people distanced themselves as soon as they heard I was a Vinnie Boy. I hated letting anybody know I was from an institution, but it did help when I was about to be picked on. Bullies were afraid that if they started something with one Vinnie Boy they would have to deal with all of us.

Vinnie Boys got their candy at Pop's, where everything was enclosed in glass cases because kids tried to steal the merchandise. We had a bad reputation in the community and most of the kids would not go to Pop's if they saw Vinnie Boys inside. Like the neighborhood around SJH in Rockaway Park, the surrounding community thought we were all bad kids. It was funny because one block away youngsters were selling drugs and those streets were off-limits for Vinnie Boys.

We could not leave the building for any reason except to go to school, unless we had a written pass from the dormitory counselor. Bitter battles erupted between the counselor who guarded the front door and the kid who wanted to leave but did not have a pass. I think the front door coverage was the worst job a counselor could have, because he was standing in the way of an adolescent boy's freedom. That unenviable task was usually assigned to a burly counselor, but it did not really matter, because if a boy lost the argument to get out of the building legitimately, he could usually sneak out through the back door and climb over the fence.

The Crusaders

Football was very important at the home, and there was a lot of pride and tradition among the St. Vincent's Crusaders. In fact, education took a backseat to football—both the staff and the kids viewed classwork as a poor second to what happened on the gridiron. St. Vincent's Home had three teams—Pee Wee (thirteen- to fifteen-year-olds), Intermediate (fifteen- to sixteen-year-olds), and Junior Division (sixteen- to eighteen-year-olds). As each team had only twenty-five players, competition was fierce. Everyone wanted to be picked and be part of the "in crowd."

At fifteen, my eyes were weak and my athletic coordination was poor. I got teased by the other kids, but they knew they could go only so far. I earned my chops my first summer at Camp Christopher's after Harry Perez yelled, "Four eyes!" one day when I was up at bat. I was so enraged that I dropped the bat in the middle of the game and ran full blast into the center of the field, swinging my fists at him. The counselors and campers all scrambled to break it up. (Of course, the kids were not running as fast, since they wanted to see a good fight. In fact, some yelled to the counselors to "let 'em fight.") But from that day on it was known that Ed Rohs was no punk. It didn't hurt that Harry happened to be the football team's running back and one of its toughest players.

Whether it was because I had proved myself or because I was big for my age, I got accepted on the Intermediate team and after a year I was chosen to play for the Junior Division. I was on that team for the next three years, becoming a very good center on offense and tackle on defense. I had found my niche! The John Jay football coach, Mr. Boyle, and his assistant coaches, Mr. Riccio and Mr. Carbonaro, saw me in action in gym class and tried to convince me to join their team. After evading their requests for a while, I finally admitted that I could not participate in high school football because if I stayed for practice I would miss dinner at St. Vincent's, which was served only until five thirty. (Nobody had the imagination to figure out that for the price of a couple of hot dogs I would have been happy to play for their team.)

In retrospect, I regret not playing for my high school team, because it would have gotten me out of St. Vincent's and might have helped me assimilate earlier into the larger community. On the other hand, I would probably have starved.

Football became my key to survival in grimy, dangerous downtown Brooklyn. I cheered myself hoarse at games. I learned the team song and sang it on road trips. At game time I got all fired up and became a completely different person. I was proud to wear the St. Vincent's Home Crusaders blue-and-white football uniform. Think David and Goliath! The Crusaders were a ragtag team of twenty-five institutionalized kids, wearing shabby old uniforms, up against the opposing team of fifty players, each wearing a spiffy new team outfit. They had three or four coaches. We had one, but he was a cool New York City police officer named Phil Reeves. He was one of the toughest and meanest-looking people I had ever met. The entire team respected him—not just because he was a tough police officer, but also because we trusted that he took our well-being seriously. Years later, I learned that he played baseball for St. John's Prep and that his teammate had been Mario Cuomo, who would go on to serve as governor of New York State from 1983 to 1994.

And when all was said and done, we had one great advantage: our opponents were afraid of us. They thought St. Vincent's Home for Boys was a reform school for teenage thieves, murderers, and psychopaths. They were scared because they thought that even our parents had given up on us! We could hear their coach give them a pep talk: "Don't be afraid of them. They're a bunch of punks—and there's only twenty-five of them. Why are you playing like sissies?" But even though they talked trash and cursed us out on the scrimmage line, we could tell they were scared by the way they lined up. My dorm mates and I—Ratimos Rios, Ronald Carey, Jamie Melendez, John London, Harry Perez, Freddie Velez, Raul Ortega, Pablo Cintron, Carlos Melendez, John Babich—had more determination than the other teams because for some of us football was the only area where we could succeed.

Most of the teams we played were located in white neighborhoods, and I would hear racial slurs—from spectators and players alike. In one game, I was about to hike the football to the quarterback when the middle linebacker called out to me, "Hey, nigger lover." I did not understand what he was talking about. In my eyes, the guys I lived with were cool. They were my friends. I loved some of them like brothers. I was a white kid in a mostly black and Hispanic institution, but none of the kids ever directed racial epithets at *me.*

One day, as we prepare to climb on our bus after beating a team on their home turf, we see the spectators armed with rocks and yelling racist filth. We are just kids playing a game of high school football, and we are scared out of our wits. I see the crowd and I cannot believe the level of anger I hear and the hatred in their eyes. Coach Reeves tells us to walk slowly to the bus to project confidence, and to get on the bus without saying a word. He walks behind us and instructs Ratimos Rios, the team captain, to assume leadership of the group in his absence. We do as instructed but the crowd is not finished with us: they are about to start pelting the bus with rocks and bottles when, quietly, Coach Reeves opens his raincoat and displays his gun and shield. Suddenly the power shifts. Off-duty cops come out of nowhere to step up and stand side by side with Coach Reeves. There is absolute silence on the bus. The bus driver looks terrified. Then Coach Reeves speaks: "The first person to throw a rock will be arrested." A minute later, as the import of what has just happened sinks in, the cops tell the coach to join his team on the bus. They will handle the situation.

Coach Reeves climbs on board and tells the driver to take us back to the home. The coach is a very quiet and modest man by nature, and he sits quietly as we drive home. At first, we are too frightened

Charles Palagonia

Coach Phil Reeves calls an emergency meeting of the St. Vincent Crusaders to discuss the shooting death of Charles Palagonia, a seventeen-year-old former Vinnie Boy and Crusaders teammate, by a police officer. I knew Charlie well. We were both in St. Mary of the Angel Home and St. John's Home.

I will never forget that day. We meet in the athletic room. Coach Reeves, dressed in his uniform, has come directly from patrol in the 75th Precinct in Brooklyn. He looks more distressed than I have ever seen him before. Charlie Palagonia was shot at 2:00 A.M. as he climbed over roofs across the street from SVH, and Coach Reeves has left work to come and tell us the whole story.

He takes a .38-caliber bullet from his belt and passes it around to each player.

"This is the kind of bullet that killed Charles Palagonia. He should never have been out on the roofs in the middle of the night. When the police officer yelled, 'Freeze,' Charlie should have stopped. And just so you know, I spoke to the police officer from the 76th Precinct who fired the gun that killed Charlie, and when he learned that he had shot a Vinnie Boy and a former player on my team, he broke down in tears."

Then, without saying another word, the coach leaves to go back to work patrolling the streets. We stay behind in the athletic room in silence. There is nothing to say.

to speak. I am really scared, and it seems like every kid on the bus is shaking. But when we realize that the danger is past, everyone gets giddy. We cannot stop talking about our coach and the other cops who stepped forward—and about those crazy racist spectators. And as a kid who has lived in blissful ignorance of racial issues, I cannot for the life of me figure out how something as small as a Pop Warner high school football game could create all this rage.

Later that same season the same team came to play us at our home field, Red Hook Stadium, which was located in a predominately black community near the Red Hook housing projects, and there were no racial outbursts or incidents. Because we had no family or friends to cheer us on (Vinnie Boys who weren't playing didn't attend because they couldn't scrape together change to buy subway tokens), the local neighborhood came out in droves. Black spectators did not harass the visiting teams, and I noticed that when I snapped the football to the quarterback no one dared sling racial slurs. But although they were treated with respect, they still seemed very nervous and could not wait to get out of the neighborhood.

I think that if St. Vincent's did not have these teams, most of us would have fallen by the wayside. The St. Vincent's Crusaders football team was the only thing keeping us together. And although I am ashamed to admit it, there were times I thanked God that I was not black or Hispanic so that I did not have to go through the discrimination and hassles my friends experienced.

Monsignor Casey

St. Vincent's is full of surprises. One particular eye-opener happens at Sunday Mass, when Monsignor William Casey, the director, uses his authority to bully the dorm counselors in front of the boys.

Monsignor Casey was physically imposing with a stocky build and big hands that made me think he was a football player or boxer before becoming a priest. He had a commanding presence that inspired respect—or was it fear?

The first time I meet Monsignor Casey is during my last year at St. John's, when he is the main celebrant of the Mass to commemorate some event. I am the altar boy assigned to serve under him, and he invites me to assume that same role when I move to St. Vincent's. Impressed by his authority and flattered by the invitation, I accept the office and for awhile I serve in the beautiful chapel on the first floor of St. Vincent's, but after several Sundays I lose interest, in part because I am older and no longer find the Mass inspiring, and in part because Monsignor's terrible temper grosses me out. I see firsthand how he abuses his staff. Instead of the usual boring ritual, we get to watch him shriek at subordinates, which begs the question of how he expects us to respect these men when he treats them like dirt.

I remember one particular Sunday morning. Monsignor is agitated because he thinks we are not singing loud enough. Who knows why? Maybe the organist has ramped up the sound and is drowning us out. Maybe he has wax in his ears, or maybe it is because no one really wants to sing those hymns anyway. Whatever the reason, right in the middle of Mass, Monsignor Casey comes storming down off the altar. He is in a rage. He walks briskly up and down the aisle clapping his hands and screaming at us, "I can't hear you." He is yelling at the dorm counselors, "I can't hear you either. What do you think I'm paying you for? Open your mouths and sing. How do you expect the kids to sing out loud if you're not singing out loud?" He ignores the fact that some counselors are not Catholic, that they do not know the hymns, and that they could not care less.

From my perch at the back of the church near the organ, I observe everything that goes on. The kids giggle and laugh at the staff for not having the guts to talk back at him. What they do not understand is that our counselors just want to keep their jobs. After Mass, as everyone leaves the church, some of us tease the dormitory counselors and mimic the monsignor. The staff tries to escape by piling into the staff elevator, which is off-limits to us, but for days after this humiliation we go around telling the more soft-spoken counselors that they are chumps for putting up with Monsignor Casey. Of course, we don't dare pick on the tougher counselors, because although it is not supposed to happen, some of them hit us.

But back to Monsignor Casey. Once or twice, I have been asked to meet with him in his office to deal with some school issues; the office is right off his private apartment. It is the most beautiful room I have ever seen. The dark, carved, and highly polished wooden desk stands on a beautiful oriental area rug. The rug absorbs noise and the room is very quiet. On one occasion, Monsignor is called away and I peek into his private rooms. I discover that Monsignor Casey lives in lovely, spacious quarters.

What am I supposed to think? I am angry with this nasty man and envious of his elegant life. How can he live this way while we are packed in like sardines? But I also admire him. I am fifteen and I want people to fear me the way they fear Monsignor Casey. I see firsthand the advantages of instilling fear in people. But it gets even more complicated because Monsignor Casey is an excellent fundraiser. I know he has raised the money to build Camp Christopher and that every year he gets people to dig deep into their pockets to keep the place running. The camp is operated by private donations. Every summer I am there, the monsignor and his administrative staff, Robert Fitzpatrick and Louis Menachino, bring the guest of honor for the upcoming fund-raising event at the St. George Hotel to the camp and give him a grand tour. Also in attendance is an entourage of St. Vincent's powerful board members, among them the owner of the Waldbaum's supermarket chain, the senior vice presidents of the Kings County Trust Company, the Home Title Trust Company, the Ridgewood Savings Bank, and the chancellor of the New York City Board of Education. We campers wear special T-shirts that have been printed for the occasion to show how well we are being cared for and how thrilled we are to be there.

Monsignor drives around in a black Cadillac and hobnobs with rich and powerful New Yorkers, but he comes through, and it is because of him that every summer I escape from Brooklyn and get to live in the country. In the end, I have to acknowledge that although Monsignor Casey is a bully and lives like a king, he does good things, and I give up my anger.

9   Growing Pains

First Dance

When I am fifteen years old the gates to paradise open: I get to go to my first dance. It is a monthly event open to all the boys in the home, held in the St. Vincent's second-floor auditorium. Parish girls and girls from the local community are invited, and we are allowed to invite girlfriends some guys may have met at school or in the neighborhood, although most of us had not had such luck. I dream that this dance will change that for me. Oh, the excitement! Living, breathing girls. I cannot stop thinking, dreaming, fantasizing. Dancing cheek-to-cheek for the first time in my life.

But how can a fellow make a good impression and avoid giving off a deadly institutional vibe? You have to look good, which means a buzz cut hair trim from the barber who comes into St. Vincent's every two weeks. You have to look cool, which means ordering shark-skin slacks, an Italian knit shirt, and wingtip shoes from wholesale consignment. And most important, you have to smell good, which means Old Spice aftershave and deodorant. But first, you have to take a shower. Everyone has that one figured out, and on the late afternoon of the big event, the communal shower in the basement is hopping with testosterone-screaming, naked fifteen-year-old boys shoving one another aside in a frantic race to achieve an acceptable state of clean.

At this turning point in my life, as I prepare to be initiated into the mysteries of carnal delights, Sister Helen Thomas is making her rounds in the basement on the way to her domain in the kitchen. She hears a commotion in the shower room and marches in—an imposing black-clad figure, ready to do battle in a gleaming, white-tile male sanctuary.

"Get outta here, Sista!"

"Somebody make her go!"

"This is the boys' shower, Sista! Ever hear of privacy?"

This little old feisty nun who by her very nature is a ball of fire yells back, "Oh, shut up—I've seen bigger and better!" We laugh hysterically while at the same time grabbing towels to cover ourselves.

I dry myself, tie the towel around my waist, and race to the dorm, where I dress with excruciating care. Am I cool enough? Will I pass? I have agonized over how I can make myself special—different from the other guys coming to the dance with the same thought on their mind. The competition is fierce. How do I approach them? What do I say?

Jamie Melendez, Ricardo (Ricky) Colon, and Frank Barbuscio, self-proclaimed Don Juans, take it on themselves to give me all kinds of advice. They know that I am very shy and at the same time extremely excited, hoping to meet my first real girlfriend. They are really trying to look out for me and help me out. I am all ears at this exciting moment.

"Look her right in the eye and say, 'Hi, I think you're pretty. Want to dance?'"

"I can't."

"Why not?"

"I'm shy, I'll stutter."

"Look, lemme show you," says Jamie. "Pretend you're me, and I'll pretend I'm a girl." Ricky cracks up and Jamie gives him a dirty look.

"You don't have to say anything. Just pretend you're cool."

We practice, Jamie in gray sharkskin and me in blue, and for a while I am sort of OK, trying to pretend Jamie is a pretty girl and I am a handsome guy with all the moves. He bats his eyelashes and takes my hand, which cracks everybody up, and then of course it falls apart. I stammer and blush. I think, Lucky Jamie, he's got a girlfriend named Olga, who smokes expensive cigarettes and takes him away for trips. She has promised that he can move in with her when he turns eighteen. He does not understand why I am afraid that those girls will know that nobody really wants me.

The dance takes place in a large room that serves as a meeting hall, barbershop, laundry pickup, and movie theater. Today it is a dance hall, but there is no fruit punch, pretzels, or corn chips. No cookies, Coca-Cola, ice buckets, or candy. There are no soft lights or balloons attached to red-and-yellow crepe paper hanging from the fifteen-foot ceiling . . . Just unpadded metal folding chairs in a semicircle, making a tinny sound whenever they are moved on the hardwood, darkly polished floors, bathed in institutional yellow fluorescent lighting.

On the way up to the second floor to meet the girls, I notice two burly staff members standing guard in front of the stairwell, like gestapo agents, planted to make sure nobody tries to sneak a girl into the dorm. We swagger past them, enjoying a momentary surge of macho pride just knowing they think we pose a threat on that score. Entering en masse, we are scrubbed, combed, slicked, primed with aftershave—and terrified. The girls stand lined up against the wall—prisoners before a firing squad in pencil-thin skirts, black flats, low-cut blouses—pink, blue, yellow, green—and hair that's been teased, sprayed, and adorned with shiny barrettes. We stand on the opposite wall, and as we appraise one another they giggle.

Why are they laughing? Are they nervous—or are they laughing at me? The glaring lights make our dance floor look like a prison lockdown. I take a closer look at the girls. Maybe they are giggling because they, too, are nervous. Why are they nervous? They are nervous because they want to impress me! OK. Here goes.

"Hi—my name is Ed Rohs. What's yours?"

Silence. I wait expectantly. I would take a first name, even a whisper. What's the matter with her anyway? Why is she giggling?

Blushing and giggling. On the other hand, she is not running away. Emboldened, I manage to get my arm around her waist the way I had been taught, and then, oh my God, we are dancing! Blushing and giggling, but dancing. Away we go! Little Anthony and the Imperials sing "Two Kinds of People."

My heart soars. She has beautiful features, like my Aunt Katherine, which is not a bad thing, except that at this moment I do not want to think about Aunt Katherine. I would like to think about kissing my partner's pretty mouth and nibbling at her pink lipstick. Then she speaks to me!

"Why are you in this place?"

I don't know what to say. The truth is, I am very shy and tongue-tied with longing.

"What did you do? Did you rob someone?"

This girl thinks I am a robber!

"My mother says you're all juvenile delinquents."

Thanks a lot, lady.

Now I am sweating. And as I make my way around the floor, Ricky passes me, looking cool and slick, dancing with a pretty little Latina. I bet *she's* not acting like his parole officer.

Little Anthony finally shuts up. I return her to the bullpen and, fleeing back to the dance floor, bump backward into a little girl—she must be four feet tall! She looks terrified, but I grab her and we start to dance to "Blueberry Hill."

Suddenly, she lets out a little cry and runs from the room, leaving me alone on the floor.

My next conquest actually smiles and tells me her name. Wonder of wonders, Carmella lets me hold her close as we dance to the Five Satins' "In the still of the night."

I inhale her perfume. This is what heaven is like. That's the last thing I remember thinking before Sister Helen Thomas swoops down.

"Ed Rohs," she yells out. "What are you doing? Leave room for the Holy Ghost."

No room for the Holy Ghost.

Stricken, Carmella whispers, "I'm sorry, Sister," and disappears. She takes with her what I am sure is my last chance for happiness. I shoot Sister Helen Thomas a look that says, "Look what you did now."

John Jay High School

I enter John Jay with the expectation that I will broaden my horizons. In a way I am right, and my four years there are eye-opening, to say the least.

For the first time in my life, I am in a coeducational school. Even if I do not speak to the girls, at least I can look at them all day long—in class, homeroom, and in the hallways between classes. And sometimes, if I am lucky, I can catch a glimpse of leg as they walk down the staircase.

I am also part of the larger community and receive some extra-curricular lessons about race. I see white kids sitting on one side of the cafeteria and blacks and Hispanics on the other. I have grown up being in the minority and I know a lot of Hispanic guys from St. Vincent's who go to John Jay, so it is natural for me to sit with them. Until this moment, it has not mattered to anyone, maybe because we are all in the same boat. Growing up in Catholic institutions, where a kid's ethnicity is the least of his problems, we are color-blind. Until now, I had never seen guys segregate themselves based on their color. I get some strange looks from both sides of the cafeteria, and someone finally asks me why I am not sitting with "my kind." I tell him that I was never taught to do that, and they look at me like I am from Mars.

I am totally out of sync with my surroundings. On my first day at John Jay, I go to the lunchroom with the lunch pass I receive from my dorm counselor. The other students on line put food on their tray as they make their way to the cashier, but I don't know what I'm supposed to do so I don't take anything. When I get to the cashier, she asks me why I don't have food on my tray for checkout. I hand her the lunch pass, and she yells to the other kitchen help, "St. Vincent welfare lunch. Give him the meal."

Let me die now, God. Please let me die.

I can feel my face turn beet red. I want to crawl under the counter. But I go back on line and get my free "welfare lunch." When I finish eating I run out of the cafeteria, and for the next two years I walk home from school so I can cash in my subway token for money to buy a buttered roll instead of getting the welfare lunch. I tell friends I am not really hungry, although for the next two years I starve. Eventually I realize I am being overly sensitive. No one cares where I live, and, besides, I am hungry!

Playing Hooky

In freshman year, I begin to cut my English class, which I have right after homeroom. Coincidentally, my homeroom teacher, Mr. Weeks, is also my English teacher. One day during homeroom attendance he yells out in front of the entire class, "Eddie Rohs, how do you have the nerve to come to my homeroom class every day and then not show up for English? I'm not blind, and I'm going to have to call your parents on you. See me at the end of homeroom."

We meet and he asks for my parents' names and phone number. My response is, "Mr. Weeks, I have no mother and father, I live at St. Vincent's Home." His face shows complete shock and he immediately softens his approach. Instead of yelling, he counsels me about the importance of going to school. I do not remember exactly what he says, but I do remember leaving the class thinking that he was on my side; from that day on, no matter what shenanigans I pull in other classes, I never cut Mr. Weeks's English class again.

I recently visited my good friend Dr. Henry Floyd in his office on Boerum Place, where St. Vincent's still stands. Henry came to the home in September 1965 as a dormitory counselor, and forty-five years later, having received his master's and doctoral degrees, he is now the vice president and associate executive director at the home.

That day, Henry's office was piled high with books and end-of-year reports. We chatted about the old days, and the topic came around to the way Vinnie Boys had been raised. I asked him what he remembered about how the boys related to their high school. He pointed out that many of the boys at St. Vincent's were unused to the big, impersonal New York City public schools. Some dealt with their fear and insecurity by cutting a class, as I did, while others simply skipped school altogether. He told me that truancy was such a big problem that one St. Vincent's staffer had been assigned to make phone calls to each high school with Vinnie Boys to check their attendance.

"Truancy? It is no surprise. You raise a kid in a closed institution. He attends small Catholic schools on the grounds where he lives. He knows his classmates—he probably even knows his teachers. No wonder, if you take him out of that environment and throw him into a school with a couple of thousand kids he's going to have some problems. Added to the dislocation is the shame of being in an institution when everyone else has a proper home."

His comment reminds me that in my homeroom, all fourteen St. Vincent boys gave different addresses on State Street, because no one wanted to admit in public that he was a Vinnie Boy.

As for me, I can see now that cutting my homeroom teacher's class was a cry for help. I will never forget Mr. Weeks and his sensitivity and kindness to me when everything was going wrong.

In Harmony

Ricardo Colon and Frank Barbuscio are buddies from SJH who came to St. Vincent's, and Jamie Melendez, a new kid I meet at St. Vincent's, came via St. Agnes Home, up in Sparkill, New York. To help pass the time, we form a singing group and perform what people now call the "oldies but goodies." We practice harmonizing in the hallways, stairwells, and wherever else the tile walls amplify our voices. Frank sings tenor, Jamie alto, Ricky baritone, and I sing bass.

We are good and so sometimes we are invited to sing at the monthly dances and bingo fund-raiser held at the Grand Prospect Hall. But we receive the ultimate accolade when St. Vincent's asks us to perform at their annual fund-raising dinner at the old St. George Hotel in Brooklyn Heights, the Monday before Thanksgiving.

Now that we are the public face of St. Vincent's Home, Monsignor Casey and the board do not want us going around looking like a bunch of orphans! So they give us money to buy performance clothes, and one Saturday morning the four of us race over to the Abraham & Straus department store on Fulton Street.

This is a new experience. Until the moment I enter the dressing room and experience the bliss of choosing my own outfit, absolutely everything I wear (except for Aunt Katherine's gifts) is purchased wholesale and in bulk. In St. Vincent's Home, the vendors arrive and place their items on cafeteria tables for the kids to make their selection. The coat vendor comes to visit with raincoats in three colors—black, brown, or olive green. The shoe vendor has black, brown, and cordovan Oxfords. There is a dress pants vendor and a belt vendor. In all my nineteen years raised in institutions, except for my short time living with the Grimmers, I have never shopped for anything more significant than an ice cream cone.

So here we are, four Vinnie Boys in shopping heaven. Like young men in the outside world, we receive permission, within budget, to choose the clothes we like. Not surprisingly, we end up purchasing the teen uniform of the day: gray sharkskin slacks, blue Oxford button-down dress shirts, red cardigan pullover sweaters, dress socks, black leather belts, and Oxford wingtips. These clothes are a cut above anything we ever owned before. The slacks and shirts are well tailored, the sweaters are soft wool instead of a synthetic blend, the socks are silky, and the shoes are beautiful black Italian leather. We look like a professional singing group And we feel like a million dollars.

We sing "Gloria," "Just Two Kinds of People in the World," and "Oh, What a Night." Vinnie Boys think we are cool. Life is looking up. We are invited to parties in people's homes where we perform for money, and our dorm counselor gives us special passes to stay out after curfew. But then things suddenly turn dark. One evening we arrive with our dates to perform at a party on Sackett Street in downtown Brooklyn. We dance and then we perform, and at around eleven thirty we leave with our dates and go around the corner to Union Street to wait for the 5th Avenue bus. To pass the time and impress our girlfriends we start singing, which turns out to be a big mistake.

Neighborhood kids appear from nowhere and attack us with their fists and with bottles, sticks, and garbage cans. Anything they can throw gets hurled at us and we run for our lives. My date is screaming hysterically and when her shoe slips off I swoop her up in my arms and run across the street on 5th Avenue back to the apartment around the corner where we had performed. The hooligans pursue us, yelling racial slurs and throwing bottles and garbage cans in our direction. It feels like they want to stomp us to death. As we race to safety, my date screams, "I need my shoe," to which I yell back,

Ricardo Colon

Ricky Colon and I had a shared history. We both went to St. John's and St. Vincent's. We both were on the football team and, of course, the singing group. He was an outgoing, charming guy, tall and lanky, with matinee idol looks that brought the girls to him in droves. He spoke Spanish fluently, which was a rarity because every home I went to discouraged us from speaking any language except English. And he was more street-smart than any of the other guys. When he was not going to school, playing football, or singing in our group, Ricky loved hanging out on the street. And even though I envied him—I was a stocky kid with two left feet and Coke-bottle glasses—we were close friends. He was kind to me and tutored me in the mysterious ways of the opposite sex.

After we graduated, I lost touch with Ricky, although I saw him from time to time hanging out in downtown Brooklyn, always with a bevy of girls vying for his attention. They were all high on drugs. It was the mid-1960s and drugs were rampant and easily available. Ricky Colon got caught up in it. Over time, I saw him deteriorate. My efforts to convince him to receive drug treatment went in one ear and out the other.

A few years later, Ricardo Colon made the front page of the *Daily News*. He confessed to stabbing his girlfriend seven times, wrapping her in aluminum foil, and storing her under his bed until he could not take the stench and turned himself in. It was an awful crime, and an awful end for a sweet and charming guy.

But today, when I think of Ricky, I remember a kid with a strong, sweet voice harmonizing "In the Still of the Night" under a streetlight on a Brooklyn corner.

"To heck with the shoe. I'll buy you another one. Your life is more important than a shoe." She is getting heavy. I stagger as I try to get us to safety. Then, thank God, I hear police sirens.

We tell the cops that we are from St. Vincent's and that we were singing while waiting for the bus. They call the home for someone to come and pick us up, and then they explain that tensions in the neighborhood are high because Hispanics are moving into the neighborhood. Mr. McGinley, the childcare director, drives up and escorts us back to safety at St. Vincent's after bringing our dates back to their homes. It is the last time we sing on any street corners. Eventually we disband our singing group and focus on football.

Summer in the City

At the end of my junior year I am not allowed to return to Camp Christopher. This is the summer I prepare to leave the Catholic home nest by finding summer employment and living on my own. I am really upset, but they tell me that if I do not get a job I will be discharged from the home and forced to fend for myself. I know this is no idle threat because I have seen it happen to other Vinnie Boys.

St. Vincent's aftercare social worker finds me a summer job in Brooklyn Heights working in the mail and file rooms at the Interboro Title Insurance Company on Clinton Street, and a clean furnished room to live in on State Street between Court and Clinton. I am just blocks away from St. Vincent's. I am told that I must wear a shirt and tie, and, feeling important and grown up, I go to Fulton Street and buy affordable clothes for the occasion. I am very lucky, since most of my friends have been given jobs as manual laborers.

For my first few days on the job, I am very conscious of being from St. Vincent's Home, and I imagine that coworkers pity me. But in reality, except for the personnel director, Mr. O'Donnell, I do not think any of the other employees know where I am from. After work I run back to the institution and tell all the other kids about my great new job. For the first time I witness some jealousy from the other boys, many of whom have menial and demeaning jobs.

It turns out to be the loneliest summer of my life. For eighteen years I have lived around hundreds of kids. Now, without any warning, I am by myself. I am happy at work, but the evenings are difficult, and I find myself sad and depressed. I eat dinner at Bickford's or Horn & Hardart, both on Fulton Street. Sometimes I just buy hot dogs from a stand and take a walk before returning to my furnished room. Nobody checks up on me, I guess because they figure that if I am not calling in to complain I must be doing all right.

It is my first experience living outside an institution and I am miserable, but I keep it to myself. Even though the aftercare social worker assures me I can call if I need anything, I do not really know him. I only met him for the first time when I applied for the job and the second time for the furnished room. We have no relationship and he has more than thirty boys who need summer jobs or full-time jobs if they are leaving for good. The same goes for housing. I am also afraid that if I complain, the guys will see me as just a crybaby weakling. But I count the weeks, and then the days, before I can return to St. Vincent's and be back with my buddies.

In the meantime, to stay sane I meet former SJH kids on the beach at Rockaway Park. Now that we are working, we all have some money and can now go on any ride we want. We go swimming and have fun looking at girls in their bikinis. We make a pact to meet every Saturday on the beach, and for a while we do. I also visit Aunt Katherine, but I tell her everything is going fine. I know she senses that something is wrong because she keeps questioning me, but I only tell her about the things that are going well. Another reason to visit Aunt Katherine on weekends is that these are the only times I get a decent meal.

Only weekdays remain bleak. I am surprised to realize that even though I am living in posh Brooklyn Heights, and even though returning to St. Vincent's means living in an open dormitory with twenty-four other boys with just a bed, a folding chair, and a small locker with my Master combination lock, I long to return. It beats being out on my own.

Harry Perez

The summer before we began our senior years, the guys in my dorm started hearing horror stories about how St. Vincent's dumped some kids after their junior year. Suddenly, I recalled seeing older SVH boys hanging out on the corner up the block from the home. What could it mean? Who among us would be shut out?

I later learned that the home might discharge a resident before his eighteenth birthday if he was doing poorly in school or making a habit of cutting class; if dormitory counselors and social workers viewed him as a troublemaker; or simply if they were afraid of him. Naturally, I was on pins and needles until the end of the summer, when I received word from my social worker, Mr. Daniel Hayes, that I was approved to stay at St. Vincent's during my senior year. I would not be discharged early. I immediately called Aunt Katherine and gave her the great news.

There was a rumor that the newer social workers were gung ho on reuniting as many kids as possible with their biological families, even if there had been no contact for years. At the end of our junior year, eight Vinnie Boys were placed on a new social worker's caseload, and they were all discharged. Harry Perez was one of these kids.

Harry was told to pack his bags and go to his father, whom he had not seen in some time. When he arrived at his dad's roach-infested one-bedroom apartment, the man invited him to sleep on the couch in the living room. But he did not have room to accommodate his son, and he did not make plans of any kind for Harry because the social worker had not contacted him beforehand to let him know that his son was coming to live there.

Harry wanted to complete his senior year at Chelsea Vocational School, the Manhattan school he had attended for the past three years, but his dad's apartment was too small and the accommodations too limited for Harry to successfully complete his senior year studies there.

When I met him to talk about his predicament, we were both in summer jobs and he had only a few days to work things out. Harry looked like he was about to break down and cry, and we decided that together we would go to his social worker and plead his case. But when we get to the home, we are told that Harry cannot enter because he has been discharged. I can enter anytime I want, but Harry is not even allowed on the fist floor to see his social worker.

Anyone with less resilience and determination than Harry might have given up, but Harry had a plan. For two days, he constantly called John McGinley, who was the director in charge of the dormitory counselors. Eventually, McGinley returned his call. Harry's perseverance won the man over and an exception was made in his case. He was told to pack his bags and come back to St. Vincent's for his last year. The only drawback was that Harry's bed had already been given to another boy, so he had to live in a dormitory with residents two years younger.

When Harry arrived in the building with his black garbage bags, all his friends raced up and down along the floor, hooting and celebrating his return. Harry confided in me that for the first time in his life he believed in angels.

Graduation

I graduate from John Jay High School with a general, non-Regents diploma. I am ashamed of myself—ashamed of a diploma that limits where I can go in the world, ashamed of my poor grades, and mostly ashamed of my failure to prove that I am not a loser. I do not go to my graduation and I do not tell Aunt Katherine. She finds out after the fact. I tell her I did not go because I did not have family to invite. To this day I remember her hurt face.

"What am I, Eddie? A bump on a log?" She is really devastated, and I add this to my list of things about which I am ashamed. Not an auspicious beginning to my new life.

It has taken me years to understand how lucky I was to have Katherine McCarthy in my life. I realize now, more than I ever did when I was a young man, that if I had not come up to her that afternoon, brashly demanding to know her name, I might have missed the miracle of knowing someone who treated me as if I were special. She singled me out from the others. I would never have received birthday cards, those wonderful cookies from Abraham & Straus, the Thanksgiving, Christmas, and Easter meals, and those gifts. It is as if she understood that I needed someone who would say, "This one, he's special. He's my Eddie."

IV

On My Own

I spake as a child, I understood as a child, I thought as a child: but when I became a man, I put away childish things.

1 Corinthians 13:11

10

Alone in the Real World

A Sentimental Journey

On a sunny, unseasonably mild January afternoon in 2009, I take a sentimental journey on the D train, ending up in Flatbush. As I exit the subway at Newkirk Avenue, I wonder if the old neighborhood has changed. I pass familiar streets. Turning left, I keep walking until I am one block past Glenwood Road and then turn onto Waldorf Court. And yes, the homes on the block look as grand as ever—American and Dutch colonial, Tudor and Victorian, each with its own manicured lawns. Many of them still have beautiful wraparound porches on double lots.

Suddenly, I am standing in front of 27 Waldorf Court, the first place I lived after the system unceremoniously dumped me out into the world. The funny thing is that nothing has changed. How could that be? After forty-five years, 27 Waldorf is still a beautiful three-story white stucco single-family house, with lovely stained glass windows in the enclosed porch. I wonder, Does the house still have those beautiful carved wood banisters that go up to the second floor and those beautiful parquet floors and Oriental rugs? Is the third floor still let out as furnished rooms, a poor relation to the rest of the house? Is it still marked by plain linoleum and painted furniture?

Standing in front of that house, I remember the morning I was discharged from the Catholic orphanage system into a world I was totally unprepared to handle.

Life on Waldorf Court

The face of the kindly aftercare social worker registers shock as I walk down the steps of St. Vincent's carrying a half-filled garbage bag. He is in the SVH's station wagon, waiting to drive me to my destination, and he expects to see me lugging cartons of adolescent junk—trophies, records, and so forth—but that black garbage bag contains every single item I own in the world. I guess some of the other Vinnie Boys that Mr. Dempsey has transported over the years had bundles of clothes they bought with money from part-time jobs here and there. All I have is one plastic bag filled with khakis and blue jeans, underwear and socks, toothbrush and toothpaste, T-shirts, and the sharkskin slacks that are my pride and joy. Under my arm, I carry three LPs but no record player to play them on.

Station wagon? A VW Beetle could have easily done the job. Away we go, with Mr. Dempsey talking a mile a minute about this and that, filling up the silent space between us. What is there for me to say? I am scared out of my wits. As we swing left onto Atlantic and then right onto Flatbush Avenue, the station wagon rolls past the main plant of Ebinger's Bakery. For the first and only time on this trip, I speak up: "Wow, so this is where St. Vincent's got those crummy pastries!" Then I retreat into my shell.

I know exactly what will happen when we arrive at our destination. Once again, former Vinnie Boys have already given me the worst-case scenario. I will be abandoned in a dumpy furnished room in a crummy neighborhood. Then I will spend the rest of my life slaving away at some awful job.

We drive up Flatbush Avenue, past looming, gothic Erasmus Hall High School and the quaint Dutch Reform Church across the street. Mr. Dempsey makes a turn onto Newkirk Avenue. Hey, wait a minute! Mr. Dempsey must have made a wrong turn. This is not a dump. In fact, the car is cruising along past tree-lined streets with some of the most beautiful homes I have ever seen—the picture-perfect Christmas card homes an orphan dreams about.

I am in a daze. Mr. Dempsey continues to chat, pointing out the subway station I will use to take to work. We stop in front of a lovely building on a charming dead-end block. "This is it, Eddie," he says. "Hop out. Welcome to 27 Waldorf Court."

Mr. Dempsey introduces me to my landlady—an Italian woman with red hair. She immediately begins a recitation of the house rules: no visitors, no loud noise, no telephone, no cooking facilities, no re-frigerator . . . on and on. I know about rules. My introduction to every home I have ever lived has been a litany of rules. This, at least, is familiar.

My landlady lives on the ground floor, and it is decorated beau-tifully, with lovely Victorian furniture; there are wainscoted walls and a baby grand piano draped with a gorgeous, colorful shawl. An area rug reveals sections of an old but beautifully polished hardwood floor. This is heaven. We climb the carpeted stairs from the first floor to the second. On the stairway between the second and third floor the carpeting is replaced by plain green linoleum.

I enter a clean, spare, nicely furnished room. This is mine! She tells me it is a quiet house. The reason for this, I later discover, is that most tenants are elderly. She shows me the communal third-floor bathroom, and then, suddenly, it is time to say good-bye. Jack Dempsey shakes my hand and wishes me good luck. He gives me a week's supply of subway tokens and tells me I can count on him if I need anything. He says that all I have to do is pick up the phone or drop by his office. Then he is gone. St. Vincent's Home for Boys has fulfilled its final obligation. I am free to live the rest of my life as I choose. Now what am I supposed to do?

By Myself

My landlady gives me a key and then she is gone, too. I stand still. I listen to my heart pound. Then, slowly, I look around. My room is furnished with a twin bed, a night table, a small closet, and a dresser.

The walls and ceilings are all painted white, which is a nice change from institutional green. I have white window curtains and white shades on the window. The linen is also white: white sheets, white towels, a white hospital-type bedspread, and a gray military-type blanket. And for the first time in my life, I have a lamp so I don't ever have to use the overhead light, which reminds me too much of institutional lighting. My room faces the front of the house, but because I am so high up all I see are rooftops and the tops of trees. It is hot, bright, and sunny—just a bare furnished room, but quite an improvement over my former life.

And yet, after I unpack my few belongings and check out the communal bathroom, I realize with a sinking feeling in my stomach that I am alone and isolated. The landlady will not let me have a phone. There is no refrigerator for snacks. She has not provided me with a hot plate, so I will not be able to heat a can of soup. I feel just like I did during my short stay with the Grimmers, and the summer I worked after my junior year in high school. I am cut off from my friends and the only life I have ever known, only this time it is for keeps. Nothing will be different in two weeks or at the end of the summer. Or ever. This is it.

Will I ever get out of here? Will I ever get anything for myself? I want to smash my fist through the white wall of this empty furnished room. Dammit! I deserve better. But I catch myself before I can do any damage. I am sensible enough to know that if I destroy this landlady's property she will throw me out and then where will I go? I will be too embarrassed to go to Aunt Katherine. Aside from her, my only connections are at St. Vincent's, but I have promised myself that I will never return to that place hat in hand. I will never become one of the walking wounded who returns after discharge looking for help—or a handout. I will never be the Vinnie Boy the other kids, themselves frightened of the outside world, whisper about—"Couldn't make it on his own. He's back."

So, with the survival skills I have used my whole life, I begin to strategize. I will use my first paycheck to buy a small television, and with the next paycheck, a radio. From there I will just have to figure it out as I go along. I spend the next day walking around my new Flatbush neighborhood, soothing myself by observing the solid beauty of the surrounding streets, enjoying the quiet Sunday calm and the prosperity. I breathe the sweet air, and I am reminded of my experience at St. John's, when I lived just six blocks away from beautiful homes by the ocean and people whose lives were so different from my own that I could not even begin to imagine what they were like.

Do the people who live here think I'm one of them when I walk up and down their streets, or is it written all over me that I'm from an orphanage? What will they think when they find out that the guy passing them on the street is an orphan who lives in a furnished room without a dime in his pocket, just a stone's throw away?

On Sunday I take the train to downtown Brooklyn because I want to practice going to my new job, which was set up for me while I was still at St. Vincent's. I never interviewed for this job, and I have no idea where it is or why I have been hired. What will my boss expect of me when I arrive? Is it something I know how to do? Is it something I want to do? In fact, nobody has ever sat down with me to discuss what I wanted to do with my life once I left the system.

My whole life I have always been fed, clothed, and educated. In exchange, I have had to accept the control and discipline meted out by an overworked staff. So, at nineteen, I know how to take orders. But aside from joining the armed forces (which is out of the question because of my poor vision), I don't know how far that skill set will take me.

The year before I graduated I asked Joseph Moran, the social work supervisor, if he could advise me about college. His response was swift and dismissive: "College is not for everyone."

I got it. Mr. Moran thought I was stupid. I was an underachiever who did not have a chance. All I could do was clench my fists and make a solemn promise to myself: *Mr. Moran, one day I will prove you wrong!* But, having no idea how to go about achieving that goal,

I keep doing what I know how to do, which is doing what I am told. So, on the Monday following my discharge, I begin my job working as a stockroom clerk at Home Title Insurance Company at 51 Willoughby Street.

Working on My Own

Home Title Insurance Company is located just a few blocks from St. Vincent's. It is very weird to be so close to the home and at the same time cut off from everything going on inside its walls. I can hear the PA system blaring orders I am not allowed to follow. A year ago I would have laughed myself silly if anyone had suggested that I would feel somehow rejected, that I would long for the order and the rules of the institution. But a year ago I was not living on the outside, looking in.

My first day on the job I arrive bright and early, dressed in my new dress shirt and tie. I want to make a good impression. I am sent to personnel, where everybody is polite and affable. In all my years on this earth I have never said good morning to so many people! And I can hear them whispering, "He's the new stockroom boy," but nobody says, "He's a Vinnie Boy." I am the new stockroom boy!

I love my new identity. I stand a little straighter and smile a lot more. My supervisor, Ed Gray, a former longshoreman, takes me downstairs to my workplace in the basement, a large, dreary room, and introduces me to my three coworkers: Mrs. Helen Archer, Joseph Garrity (another retired longshoreman), and John Summer, who is a few years older than I am. Mr. Gray, a tough-looking Irishman, turns out to be one of the nicest human beings I have ever met. He has a magnificent voice and sings Irish songs to break the monotony. He treats all his employees like we are part of his family. I am young and strong, so I get to do most of the heavy lifting when stationery supplies arrive and cartons of printing forms are delivered from Greco Printing Company. And even though I work in the stockroom, I am pleased to be in a business environment, where I get to wear a tie and where people treat me with respect. And while I am stocking shelves, filling out requisitions, and making copies, I am also learning as much as I can about the strange new world of business. I am all eyes and ears.

The boss knows I am from St. Vincent's Home but he never makes me feel uncomfortable. In fact, he confides in me that one of the assistant vice presidents, Tony Cirello, is also a former Vinnie Boy. When I eventually meet Mr. Cirello, I learn that he was instrumental in getting me the job in the first place, that when he heard of the job opening he called Jack Dempsey and asked if he had any good kids who needed a job. He is the first Vinnie Boy I have ever met who has made a success of himself. Until now, I have only heard about the ones who were in jail or hanging out on the street, getting high.

I visit Aunt Katherine to tell her about my experiences. She is a wonderful listener and lets me speak without interruption, my enthusiasm bubbling like fizzy champagne. She says, "You lucked out. All bosses aren't like yours." And when I go to the Court Terrace Lounge, a local bar near St. Vincent's Home, to meet the guys who graduated with me, I hear horror stories about their miserable factory work with terrible bosses. My black and Hispanic friends tell me I have a nicer home and a better job because I am white. Sad to say, they are probably right, and although I do not see a stockroom job as particularly grand, it's a start.

I have money to eat and pay my rent, but I still do not know how to live in the real world. Independent living skills were never taught in the orphanage. The system did everything for me; the only thing they demanded was obedience. I never had the chance to learn by observing how people accomplish their daily tasks, because nobody in the institutions where I lived was particularly keen on having a bunch of boys watch them while they did their jobs. Shopping for food? Cooking? Laundry? Paying for rent? Utilities? Budgeting money? Out on my own, I do not have a clue. To make matters worse, I am extremely shy, withdrawn, and very concerned that people will think I'm stupid. I am afraid to enter a supermarket (which doesn't matter while I live on Waldorf Court, since my landlady will not let me have a refrigerator and I have no place to store the food). I eat all my meals in big cafeterias—Bickford's, Horn & Hardart—both of which are conveniently located on Fulton Street, midway between Home Title Insurance and St. Vincent's. Yes, although theoretically I live on Waldorf Court, I still think of St. Vincent's as my home.

Girlfriends

Kori is a beautiful, bright, and energetic young Hispanic woman who works for the personnel director. I cannot keep my eyes off her, and keep coming up with excuses to go to Personnel. Initially, I am extremely shy, but after a while I get up the courage to ask her to go out on a date. And when Kori says yes, I am on cloud nine. I cannot stop thinking about her, and although I know better, I find a thousand more reasons to stop at her desk. I find it difficult to do my job and cannot wait for Saturday to come. I am nineteen and this is my first real date.

Kori lives in a very cool area of Brooklyn, on Eastern Parkway near Grand Army Plaza. It is close to a European-style boulevard and not far from the Brooklyn Botanic Garden, the beautiful main branch of the public library system, and the Brooklyn Museum. For our first date, I wear my best clothes and take her to Armando's, a fancy Montague Street restaurant in Brooklyn Heights that I often pass on my lunch break. I hope we can walk along the promenade and look at the romantic Manhattan skyline across the river. I am very shy and terribly nervous, but we have a good time.

I don't dare kiss her or do anything that might destroy the moment. I bring her home after midnight, and miraculously, she agrees to see me again. We really enjoy each other's company and start going out steadily. In time we develop a very intimate relationship, seeing each other every weekend and eventually during the week as well. We go to the promenade in Brooklyn Heights, to the Albee Square and RKO movie houses, and Prospect Park. I feel good about myself, probably for the first time in my life. I am not as shy as I was when we first met, and my confidence and self-esteem increase tenfold.

Aunt Katherine and Sister Johanna see Kori as the answer to their prayers. I have found a girl and I am in love! I introduce her to Aunt Katherine, and she is thrilled to see that Kori is refined and polished. They expect me to settle down, and after I confess to Kori that I am an orphan and she does not break it off, I begin to hope that maybe there is a chance she will want to marry me.

One day, about seven months into our relationship, Kori calls me from her desk and says it is urgent that we meet after work. *Why does she need to meet me? Is she pregnant?* At five o'clock that afternoon we meet in a coffee shop near the office, the kind with red leatherette booths and a white counter. We are nervous and uncomfortable. We order coffee. When it arrives neither of us takes a sip. Like a mantra I keep repeating, "Honey, what's the problem?" Finally she speaks.

"I can't see you anymore."

"What?"

"We have to break up."

"Why?"

"I need time to think."

I can't believe what I'm hearing, and my mantra changes to "What did I do wrong? I am so sorry. Whatever it is I am sorry." I repeat it over and over.

"It's not you, it's me. I need some time and space. I can't explain."

I beg her not to break up with me. I tell her she is my whole life. I dream of her every night and look forward to seeing her every day. And now, all of a sudden, she's dropping me? What am I going to do? Right there in the coffee shop, with Kori looking miserable and the waitress looking bored, I weep uncontrollably.

To this day I do not have words to describe the pain of that rejection. For the first time in my life I allowed myself to fall in love. And then, in the blink of any eye, it was over. I see there is no way to talk her out of it. Tears pouring from my eyes, I pay the cashier and leave the restaurant and walk away from Kori.

Katherine and Johanna wait for me to tell them good news, and when that does not happen at Christmastime, they look forward to Easter. But by Easter they know something bad has happened because I am no longer talking about her, and in fact, I am very subdued all through dinner. They both know better than to say anything directly, although later Sister Johanna says, "Obviously my prayers were not answered."

After the breakup, I cannot function. I don't know if my boss and coworkers suspect that we have broken up, but they are understanding and very supportive. At any other place, they would probably have sacked me for slacking on the job. But I am blessed because in this office the boss makes everybody feel like family, and in a family, I am discovering, everyone rallies around the one in need. They treat me kindly, but they are aware that I am not functioning with the energy and enthusiasm with which I used to approach my tasks. They ask if anything is wrong, and I tell them there is not. They ask if there is anything they can do, and again, of course, there is not.

It takes me about three weeks to pull myself together, and after that, I want nothing more to do with Kori; in fact, I do everything possible to avoid passing her desk. I vow that this will never happen again. This is the last time in my life that I will let a woman get close to me. About a month after the breakup, Kori calls and asks if we can resume our relationship, as though nothing has happened. We date but it is not the same and we eventually break up.

Kori moves to California. For years after our breakup I gravitate to the phone on New Year's Eve, dial her number, and hang up when I hear her voice on the other end.

Three years later I start dating Josie, who is the aunt of my young goddaughter, Alison Passy. (I knew Alison's father from our days together at SVH. He married early and I was delighted to become a godfather.) Josie is part Irish and part Hispanic. She is pretty and spunky and loves going to movies, parks, and discos. Whereas Kori is reserved and refined, Josie is a ball of fire. We date a few times, and I even take her to one of the St. Vincent's annual fund-raising dinners at the Waldorf Astoria. She is totally impressed and eats it up. I think things are moving along nicely between us. In fact, I am starting to fall in love with Josie. *How can this be happening?* I keep reminding myself to move with caution. For this reason I do not say a word to anyone—not Aunt Katherine, or Sister Johanna, or even friends like Harry.

Josie is a lot of fun, and one warm spring night we take a ride out to JFK Airport to lie on a blanket and watch the airplanes take off and land. We think this is a real cool thing to do. We park in a lot filled with other cars near the beautiful nondenominational airport church and select a pitch-black spot to spread our blanket. We are having a really nice time when, all of a sudden, people come pouring out of the church. It seems like hundreds of people have suddenly jumped into their cars, revved up their engines, and turned on their headlights. Suddenly, the whole area is lit up like a night game at Shea Stadium. We are like deer caught in the headlights. We grab our blanket and tear out of there, laughing hysterically as we run to our car for cover. We never dreamed there would be a religious service that time of night. No matter, because we are happy.

Then one night our relationship screeches to a halt over an argument so stupid that I cannot even remember what it was about. We are driving back to her home in Jamaica, Queens, yelling at each other. I reach over and give her a slap with the back of my hand. It stops the fight. This has never happened before. In my entire life I have never struck a woman. I am ashamed and embarrassed, but it does not seem to faze her one bit. In fact, after driving in silence for a while, she says, "Ed, don't worry. It's no big deal. It's not like you hit me with an open hand."

We ride around into the wee hours of the morning, trying to sort out what has just happened. I apologize, and then I apologize again.

Josie assures me that it is no big deal. But I cannot get over my sense of shame.

I break up with Josie. In the years that follow I sometimes meet her at gatherings, but we just say hello and goodbye. I am saddened to hear, when she tells me years later, that what I did was nothing compared to her abusive husband. Over the years I enjoy many relationships with many lovely women, but I am careful to keep my distance. In time, I begin to understand the depth of the psychic damage that I experienced as a result of my parents' abandonment, and the lasting consequences of my abusive experience with Kevin and Brother D. In retrospect, I realize that both Josie and I would have benefited from clinical counseling. As a clinical social worker, I wish I had been able to give her good advice. As a fallible human being, I wish someone had given me some good advice as well.

Back to the Drawing Board

A year after I come to live in my little room in Waldorf Court, I move into my first apartment, a studio on Joralemon Street, across the street from the YMCA in Brooklyn Heights. It is a great neighborhood with lots of young working people. A milestone: I get my first phone. A bigger milestone would be if I could finally have a bathroom of my own, but it is a tiny apartment, so I am still stuck with a common bathroom in the hallway. In 1967 I give notice at Home Title Insurance Company and bounce around for a while, trying to figure out what I want to do with the rest of my life. I work in a variety of entry-level jobs: the stock transfer department of a brokerage house down around Wall Street and an over-the-counter brokerage house, among others.

But I do not much enjoy the work, and after a while I begin thinking about finding a job in the public sector. Aunt Katherine says, "Get a civil service job. I don't care if it's federal, state, or local. You'll never get rich but you'll have a good salary, a health plan, and a pension. And there is job security. Get a safe and secure job, like my dear Tom."

Her husband Tom worked as a letter carrier for the U.S. Postal Service until his death. It seems like a sensible plan so every week at the newsstand I buy *The Chief*, a publication that lists all upcoming federal, state, and local civil service examinations. It's time well spent because one day I see a civil service test for a police administrative aide (PAA) with the New York Police Department (NYPD). I have always dreamed of working in law enforcement. I pass the entrance examination, and Aunt Katherine buys us a bottle of champagne to celebrate.

I embark on a vigorous three-month-long training program at the New York City Police Academy to learn the department's criminal procedure law, penal law, and policies and procedures. And, in those precomputer days, I am required to take a typing course and show that I can type forty-five words per minute. (Aunt Katherine is tickled that I am learning to type, because she is an executive secretary for the vice president of the Ingersoll Rand Corporation's international division.)

And then, finally, I become a member of the first civilian class in the history of the NYPD. As a PAA, I am assigned to Lieutenant Thomas Bogan of the 76th Detective Squad on Union Street, whose catchment area covers Carroll Gardens, some of South Brooklyn, and Red Hook. Before the PAA was created, police officers and detectives performed clerical jobs. For more than one hundred years a mindset existed in the NYPD that only police officers could fill out forms when a citizen came in to report a crime, and only the detective squad could type up reports when an investigation was underway. Finally, policy makers realized that the City of New York could save millions of dollars by hiring civilians to do paperwork and putting police officers and detectives out on the street to do the work for which they were hired. It was a drastic change. Now, decades later,

PAAs are entrenched in the NYPD. And when I have occasion to speak to police officers either walking a beat or in a patrol car, they tell me how valuable PAAs are. Most tell me that they hate coming into the precinct to do the paperwork.

It is a great assignment. Besides typing, recording, filing detectives' arrest and investigative activities, and answering the telephone, I am on a normal Monday to Friday, 9:00 A.M. to 5:00 P.M. schedule, with holidays off. Typically, PAAs are assigned to the patrol division or the local precinct, which means they work on rotations—8:00 A.M.–4:00 P.M.; 4:00 P.M.–12:00 A.M.; 12:00 A.M.–8:00 A.M. I feel pretty lucky to have a nine-to-five shift.

Who's Your Rabbi, Rohs?

When the sergeant in the police academy announces our assignments, he stops reading from the list, turns to me, and asks "Who's your rabbi, Rohs?" I have no idea what he is talking about. I never heard this expression in my life, so in front of the entire class I ask him what he means. The class cracks up and I feel like an idiot. There is no way I can explain to the group that coming from the Catholic orphanage system, New York's streetwise, multiethnic expressions like "Who's your rabbi?" are totally alien to me. (In time, I learn that he is asking who in a position of authority is looking out for me and pulling strings to see that I get a plum assignment.)

Between 1967 and 1969 I work at the PAA job, and even though I am not a patrolman and do not have a silver or gold shield, I enjoy being close to the action. My poor vision prevents me from realizing my dream of following in the footsteps of other Vinnie Boys who went on to became police officers. But in time I learn that the five district attorney's offices throughout New York City (Kings, New York, Richmond, Queens, and Bronx Counties) all have their own detective investigative squads that work hand in hand with the city police, and that the vision requirements for these jobs are less stringent.

I also discover that the office of the Kings County (Brooklyn) District Attorney Eugene Gold has several openings, but to get on the squad frequently requires knowing someone with political pull ("Who's your rabbi?" indeed!). For the first time since leaving St. Vincent's, I contact Mr. Jack Dempsey. I figure that anybody who finds jobs for hundreds of kids as they get discharged from St. Vincent's must know a lot of people. My instincts are correct; he connects me to a former St. Vincent's and SJH alumni, the former state assemblyman and New York State Supreme Court judge Joseph Dowd. I meet him in his law office on Joralemon Street near where I live. He takes me under his wing and explains that my police administrative aide experience alone will not do the trick. I need to devote time and energy to the local Democratic club on Henry Street in Cobble Hill. Heeding his advice, I get politically involved and go down to the clubhouse several evenings a week, where I experience firsthand how our local political process works. I stuff campaign literature, attend campaign fund-raisers, and meet all kinds of politicians, lawyers, and judges. It is a great social outlet, too, and a good alternative to hanging out at a bar. Being involved in campaigning is a lot of fun. I chat with tenants while I go door-to-door soliciting signatures on a petition to get Joe Dowd reelected.

Coach Ed Rohs at St. Vincent's Home

One day my former football coach, Phil Reeves, invites me to come back as a part-time, paid football, baseball, and basketball coach for the thirteen- to sixteen-year-olds at St. Vincent's Home. He has more confidence in me than I have in myself, and he convinces me that I have the leadership skills and discipline needed to lead the football team to victory in the Pop Warner Football Conference. I am flattered and frightened.

My biggest concerns are that my friends will think I am weak— that I cannot move on. I am scared they will point to the coaching appointment as proof that I am still dependent on St. Vincent's. Maybe I am afraid they might be right, and that I am one of those Vinnie Boys who cannot let go. I am haunted by what it would say about me. On the other hand, the possibilities are exhilarating. So, after thinking about it for a week, I put aside my fears and accept the challenge.

I coach the boys for three years and I have a blast. My team, the Mount Loretto team, and a team from the Bedford Stuyvesant section of Brooklyn are the three minority squads in the league. We play our home games on my old stomping ground, Red Hook Stadium. I discover that some things die hard—visiting teams from Queens still hate coming to our mostly African American community. Once again, I witness racial incidents when playing on the opposing team's field. On one occasion, Phil Reeves, who is now the coach of the Junior Division squad, happens to be watching a game I am coaching. In a repeat of the incident that traumatized me years before, after the game ends Phil must show his gun and raise his police shield to protect players who are being threatened.

I want to stand by him, but he tells me to go with my team on the bus. And like that time long ago, fellow police officers—spectators who have witnessed the growing hostility from the opposite side of the field—step up to the plate and stand shoulder to shoulder with him while I escort my team to the bus. Once again, I cannot believe how close we came to getting our bus bombarded with rocks and having all the windows busted. Once again, fellow officers who, until a few minutes ago were part of the crowd, step up to the plate and prevent a catastrophe.

Moving Up

For about a year after I leave St. Vincent's I spend every Friday and Saturday night at the Court Terrace Bar and Lounge, hanging out with former Vinnie Boys, drinking beer or scotch and water, and reminiscing for hours about the bad old times and the good old days.

I am still dealing with my breakup with Kori, and I find myself becoming bored and depressed. I figure out there has to be more to life than hanging out in a bar and going to clubs, where Motown music temporarily takes my mind off my shaky hold on the universe. One Saturday night I do not show up at the bar. In fact, after that night I never show up again. Some of the guys probably think I dropped dead but I don't care. I feel proud of myself for making this important decision

In exchange, through my political work and my coaching, I become acquainted with people with the intelligence and political influence to make a difference in our world. The payoff comes when, at age twenty-four, I receive a notice to be interviewed for the position of detective investigator by the chief assistant district attorney, Elliott Golden. I do well and am subsequently deputized as a peace officer, where I work from 1969 to 1972.

Gun and gold shield in hand, I am on top of the world. But the excitement wears off and I begin to appreciate the enormous responsibility I now have. Nonetheless, in reflecting on that time, I realize how immature and inexperienced I was, and I shudder when I remember the stupid things I did. Feeling invincible, I put myself in dangerous situations that before, without that gun and shield, I would have avoided.

I move again, this time into an apartment across the street from the Brooklyn Criminal Court at 125 Schermerhorn Street, which I share with Richard Rivera. Richard is a former Vinnie Boy who works as a cashier/bagger at Bohack supermarket while waiting for his appointment with the NYPD. Richard and I have a lot of shared history. Not only did we attend St. Vincent's at the same time, but we were also at John Jay High School together.

The apartment is much larger than anything I have ever lived in before, and I finally have a bathroom inside the apartment. There is also a living room, kitchenette, and bedroom. We play "shoot" to see who wins the bedroom and who sleeps on the couch. I win, so theoretically I get the bedroom. But while he is a great roommate, Ricky is definitely a Don Juan type, with more girls than any guy I had ever met (I would not have minded if he shared, but of course he never does). There are times when I find myself sleeping on the sofa in the living room so that Ricky can have the bedroom.

On August 13, 1970, as I return home from the office across the street from my home, I discover a robbery taking place right under my nose. The *Daily News* of Friday, August 14, reports it:

> Detective Edward Rohs of the Brooklyn district attorney's squad thought he had a convenient, crime-free pad when he rented an apartment across the street from his office. He is right about the apartment being close to his job. He is wrong, however, for thinking no burglar would dare work virtually under the DA's eyes.
>
> On Monday afternoon Rohs is chatting with a friend on the sidewalk in front of his apartment house at 125 Schermerhorn Street when he sees a young man carrying a suitcase down the steps of the house. The young man looks familiar, although he is not a resident . . . the suitcase looks familiar too. Racing up the stairs to his fifth floor apartment, Rohs confirmed his suspicions. A tape recorder and a suitcase were missing. With the help of two patrolmen in a radio car, he tracked down the young men a few blocks away. . . . The suspect . . . had been a neighbor of Rohs' some eight or nine years ago in Far Rockaway, Queens, the detective said.

What the paper did not report is that the kid I caught, Humberto Casiano, is the younger brother of Frank Casiano, a good friend from my St. John's and St. Vincent's days. I knew Humberto, too, and liked him, the same way I liked his brother, but we did not hang out. Humberto is another Vinnie Boy and I heard through the grapevine that he became a drug addict. What happened was that one day I was coming out of the Criminal Court and going across the street to my apartment to get something during lunch. As I crossed the street I saw someone walking out of my building carrying all kinds of stereo equipment, and it definitely looked like it came from my apartment.

To make sure I was not jumping to conclusions, I sneaked upstairs to my apartment, and sure enough, my apartment had been broken into and stuff thrown all over the place. My stereo was missing. I ran back downstairs and toward Smith Street, and I saw this person carrying my stereo over his shoulders. I ran up to him and yelled, "Stop, I'm a detective." He stopped in his tracks. When he turned around to look at me, I immediately saw that he was Frank's younger brother. I showed him my detective shield and told him he was under arrest. I was so angry that I cuffed him right there. I yelled, "What were you thinking? You think you can get away with burglarizing an apartment right across the street from the Criminal Court in the middle of the afternoon?" I was so angry that I put him in my car and drove him to the 72nd Precinct myself, all the while trying to hide my concern that I was driving a prisoner quite a distance in my two-door sedan and that he could, at any stop sign, jump out. If he bolted, I would be embarrassed, and it would be a huge humiliation for the DA's office and the police department, with lots of blame to go around.

The next day, right before I pick up Humberto to bring him back to central booking before he is transported to Criminal Court to be arraigned, I read in the *Daily News* that my good friend and singing partner Ricky Colon is in the 84th Precinct, having turned himself in for stabbing a poor young woman seven times. Two former Vinnie Boys locked up at the same time. After I read about Ricky, I am even more afraid of Humberto jumping out of the car, and I drive him to arraignment with one eye on the road and the other on my prisoner. The judge "throws the book" at Humberto and I never see or hear from him again. As for Ricky, we meet from time to time after he is released from prison.

The Sweet Life

My roommate, Richard, graduated from the New York City Police Academy and received his first assignment as a police officer in the Bronx. Eventually he got his gold detective shield. Meanwhile, I became a detective investigator in the Brooklyn DA's office and moved into a twenty-four-hour doorman building in Park Slope, right on Grand Army Plaza.

I am convinced that the only reason I am approved to get into this building is because the landlord loves the idea of having someone in law enforcement living there. Of course, it is never mentioned, but I know that before my arrival, the apartment was rented to the New York City comptroller and eventual mayor Abraham Beame, who used it as a Brooklyn pied-a-terre when he moved to a grander home in Belle Harbor. I am blocks away from Prospect Park, the Grand Army Plaza library, Brooklyn Botanic Garden, and the Brooklyn Museum. I cannot believe that I am not only keeping up with the Joneses but actually living with them!

Finally, my life is moving in a direction that offers me a chance for happiness. I am growing and maturing, while being acknowledged for things I had already accomplished. And I have a job that encourages me to learn. Working as a detective investigator gives me the opportunity to see firsthand how the criminal justice system works. Besides serving subpoenas, I am available to assist the assistant district attorneys in preparing cases. I observe firsthand the disparities in how justice is meted out. I see that those defendants who have private attorneys are more likely to receive bail (they can afford it) and have their cases dismissed. The defendants assigned legal aid lawyers are more likely to be denied bail and to not have their cases dismissed, because their lawyers are either inexperienced or overworked.

But I also discover some top-notch legal aid lawyers, outstanding public servants who could quite easily have made a lot of money working as private attorneys but who choose to represent those most needy clients and provide them with fair and professional representation. I am distressed to see that most of the people going through the criminal justice system are people of color, and that the people before whom they come seeking justice are not.

During those early halcyon years, my devotion to my Aunt Katherine and her sister, Johanna, never flagged. My visits to Sunset Park became even more festive after Vatican II liberalized its rules regarding nuns. No longer confined to the convent, Sr. Johanna was pleased to replace her gown and wimple with conservative street clothes and join Katherine and me for Christmas, Easter, and Thanksgiving dinner. I looked forward to these home-cooked dinners, in part because Katherine set the table with her best china and silverware. We had a wonderful time together, eating and laughing, and there were times we would eat so much that, after dessert was served, we would fall fast asleep in the living room. Sometimes I invited a student I was coaching over for a home-cooked meal. One of our favorite guests was Ramon Nieto. Ramon would sit in Aunt Katherine's apartment and he and Sr. Johanna, who was a great admirer of Spanish culture, would have long talks. After he graduated from Sterling High School, Ramon became a boxer, winning the New York Daily News Golden Gloves trophy and boxing with the likes of former greats Michael Moore, Juan Laporte, and Michael Martinez. Katherine and Johanna were his biggest fans. Today I am proud to be godfather to his son, Ramon Nieto, Jr.

My Family Finds Me

While I was working in the DA's office and assigned to the Brooklyn Criminal Court, I often appeared before the judge on behalf of Vinnie Boys who were arrested for some mischief. Aunt Katherine never approved. Although she understood that these homeless and abandoned

The Mincemeat Pie Caper

Each year at Thanksgiving when I visit Aunt Katherine, I consume a large slice of the mincemeat pie she cuts for me. I hate mincemeat pie, especially when it is dressed with whiskey sauce, as hers often is. But since earliest childhood the sisters have taught me to always clean my plate, no matter what is on it.

The moment of truth comes when I am twenty-five. We all assemble for our traditional Thanksgiving dinner, but something is different. Aunt Katherine is distraught. She apologizes to her sister and me because, inexplicably, there has been a run on mincemeat pies in Sunset Park, and despite her best efforts she has not been able to find one for this year's Thanksgiving dinner. What a disappointment! Would we mind having pumpkin pie instead?

Thinking to comfort her, I blurt out, "That's OK, Aunt Katherine. I am glad. I hate mincemeat pie. I can't stand putting it in my mouth and having to eat it. I love pumpkin pie." The dining room, which a second ago was bubbling with laughter and holiday camaraderie, turns as silent as a tomb. I have betrayed a ritual. I have broken a trust.

"What? You have been eating mincemeat pie for years and now you tell me you can't stand it? How come you never said anything before?" I explain that I have been trained to keep my mouth shut and never complain when somebody invites me out. Sr. Johanna has the grace to nod her head in agreement.

I am never served mincemeat pie again; from that day on, the dessert menu includes both mincemeat and pumpkin pies.

kids needed good role models and tender loving care—after all, she had done that for me—she just did not want me to do it. She told me I had already experienced too much of that world. She wanted me to gain exposure to people who had experienced positive and loving home environments. She wanted me to learn about the wonderful things in life. I did not listen and kept going on my own path.

One day, the court reporter for the *Daily News*, Harry Danyluk, who observed me working as an advocate for Vinnie Boys, said, "You're in law enforcement and you're always coming out for these kids. What's your interest in advocating on their behalf?" I explained my history, and one day I was interviewed. The court photographer took my picture and it appeared in the Sunday edition of the *Daily News* on June 6, 1971, along with an article headlined, "DA's Sleuth Plays Father at Orphanage":

> Edward A. Rohs, 25, of 20 Plaza Street, Park Slope, who grew up in St. Vincent Home for Boys . . . spends most of his spare time being a friend and pal to the boys living there now. . . . "Since I am an orphan myself, I know what it feels like to need a friend," he said. "I know how necessary it is for people to take an interest in boys at the home. . . . Occasionally I run across a boy who lives in the home and has been arrested. . . . One of these recently is a boy who was arrested on a misdemeanor charge. He is very ashamed, and told me he is sorry about what had happened."
>
> Rohs appealed to the judge before whom the lad's case came up, and asked for a conditional discharge for the boy, providing he entered a job corps program. The judge granted permission for this, and the boy entered a job corps program in Texas. Before he left for Texas, the boy told his probation officer: "Do me a big favor, and thank Eddie Rohs for what he did for me."

Soon thereafter, I am informed that somebody in the White House has read the article. Apparently, they are impressed that after I left the institutional system I went back and helped kids still inside the system, both as a coach and an advocate in criminal court. On July 26, 1971, I receive a letter from the White House. I cannot believe my eyes. President Richard Nixon is thanking me for my dedication to

working with the boys at St. Vincent's. And I am not even a registered Republican.

Several weeks later I receive a call at my desk in the Brooklyn
Grand Jury Bureau, where I had recently been transferred. "Detective Rohs, please don't hang up on me," the voice says. "It took a lot
of work to track you down. I called the main DA's office and had to
talk them into giving me permission to speak with you. I don't know
how to tell you, but after seeing your picture in the newspaper and
reading that you may be an orphan, I think I may be your uncle. My
name is William Rohs. I may be your Uncle Bill. You look so much
like my brother and with a name like Rohs and the unique spelling,
anything is possible."

I am taken completely off guard, and for a long moment I am
speechless. My first instinct is to dismiss him as a crank caller. All I
can do is take his name and telephone number and check him out. I
immediately call Elena Curella, my social worker in SJH. She knows
more about my family than anybody does. Elena works right up the
block from the courthouse, and I have kept in touch with her over
the years. I figure she will know how to handle the situation.

She suggests that I meet the caller in a neutral location, like a restaurant, and pay the bill to demonstrate my independence. I follow
her advice. When he tells me he lives in Middle Village, Queens, I sug-
gest we meet at the intersection of the Queens and Woodhaven Bou-
levards, near the Long Island Expressway at a Howard Johnson's.

Bill Rohs and his wife, Mabel, are waiting for me in the restaurant vestibule. He is wearing a well-tailored brown tweed suit, a top-
coat, and a dress hat. She is wearing a full-length mink stole and fur
hat over a lovely suit. I know immediately that they are my relatives
by the way they begin to cry as soon as they see me. As for me, this
is the first time in my life that I have ever met someone with my last
name. I do not shed a tear.

We order our meals, and the first thing I ask is "If you're truly
my family, how come you never tried to reach me before this?" And
Uncle Bill tells me a story that pretty much breaks my heart.

THE WHITE HOUSE
WASHINGTON

July 26, 1971

Dear Mr. Rohs:

Recently I read a news account of your splendid efforts
on behalf of the children of St. Vincent Home for Boys.
I understand you spend your spare time coaching the
basketball and baseball teams at the Home and that you
also take the boys on recreational outings and field trips.
Your activities are all the more meaningful since you,
yourself, grew up at St. Vincent's.

Your dedication to these lonely and sometimes friendless
boys deserves the praise and commendation of all our
fellow Americans, and I want you to know of my appreciation for your fine humanitarian concern.

With every good wish,

Sincerely,

Richard Nixon

Mr. Edward A. Rohs
20 Plaza Street
Brooklyn, New York 11238

A letter from President Nixon.

"I never knew that my brother had a son out of wedlock," he says. "Although, now that I'm thinking about it, years ago your father—my brother—he showed us pictures of his kids. It was at some kind of family gathering. Nine years after you were born your parents had twins—a girl and a boy. And we all commented that they were good-looking kids, and he responded, 'If you think they're good looking, you ought to see—' Then my brother stopped in his tracks, looked down, and put the pictures back in his wallet. Now I understand—he meant you." He tells me he hopes I will come into their lives. Mabel is crying, but I tell them, "I move very slowly. I have a hard time trusting people, and you'll have to let me go at my own pace. I have a person in my life. I call her my Aunt Katherine, and ever since I was a little boy she has been there for me every Thanksgiving, Christmas, and Easter. She will always come first."

Bill says that of course he will respect my wishes, but that he and Mabel are going to try to gain my trust and include me in the family. And so a new era begins. I pay visits to their home and learn the real story about my family. My father was the youngest of seven brothers. According to Uncle Bill, his mother (my Grandma Rohs) was a tyrannical matriarch, a staunchly anti-Catholic Lutheran who raised her sons in the faith. When they grew to manhood, the sons all married Catholic women, presumably to "get back" at their mother. All her grandchildren were raised as Catholics. But her sons remained Lutheran and attended their church every Sunday, regardless where they lived.

And I learn that I come from a family of savvy businessmen. Bill, without even a high school diploma, worked his way up in the Colonial Works Paint Company until he was appointed treasurer. He purchased five trucks and convinced the president and CEO of the company to let him start his own paint delivery company, Rohs Trucking, serving Colonial Works customers, for which he hired all his brothers, including my father.

And I find out about my father, who passed away in 1970. Bill and Mabel are hesitant to say anything about him because so much of the information is negative. As it turns out, I am the son of the kind of man Aunt Katherine would call a "ne'er-do-well and a miscreant." Edward Rohs, Sr., was a bar-hopping womanizer. He could not manage his money and was always broke; his brothers always bailed him out of one financial scrape or another. Bill hired him to drive their trucks, so he always received a paycheck. If it were not for Rohs Trucking, my father might well have ended up on the street.

Uncle Bill introduces me to a cousin, Andrew Rohs, who becomes my good friend. He tells me things about my family that my aunt and uncle were too embarrassed to reveal. I discover that I have a half brother, Billy, and a half sister, Dot, from my father's first wife, Linda, and that my mother was introduced to my father through Linda, who was her best friend. All three of them would hang out in bars on Friday night. One evening, Andy and I are driving around Long Island City. Suddenly, he stops in front of a New York City Housing Authority project and points to a building.

"That's where your mother lives."

My stomach lurches, and in that moment I am transported back to St. John's Home, back to Ms. Curella's office, hearing for the first time that my impoverished parents are living with their other children and have no interest in seeing me. Andy wants me to make contact with her, but I tell him to keep driving. And when she passes away Andy gives me the name and address of the funeral home where she is being waked. I tear up the paper. The end.

Bill and Mabel welcome me into their home and I spend many wonderful evenings in their company. They seem as pleased to educate me about my family as I am about learning about my roots. Yet as much as I enjoy their company, and as much as they go out of their way to make me feel at ease, it takes me a long time before I feel confident enough to meet other members of my family.

Two years after being introduced, I announce to my aunt and uncle that I am ready to take the next step and meet other members of my biological family. I can see that they are both elated, and one day we all pile into Bill's car and drive down to Wilmington, Delaware, to visit their only son, Robert, his wife, Peggy, and their twelve-year-old son, Timothy. I already know about Bob, how he graduated at age sixteen from a prestigious private Catholic boys school (coincidentally run by the Marianist Brothers) and received his bachelor's degrees from Fordham University and his master's in business administration from MIT.

I am a nervous wreck on the ride down. We drive over the Delaware Memorial Bridge in Bill's Chevy Impala, and as we get close to our destination I am struck by the elegance and quiet grace of the houses, each one set back from a large manicured lawn. Cousin Bob's home is a very fine white brick Cape Cod residence with blue painted shutters, and when he answers the door I find myself facing a very tall, proper-looking gentleman. Extending his hand and giving me a firm handshake, Bob puts me right at ease: "Welcome, Cousin Ed. It's a pleasure to meet you, I've heard so much about you." Then he introduces me to his wife and his son, a blond-haired kid who looks a lot like pictures of me at his age.

Cousin Bob and Peggy make every effort to put me at my ease. That Friday night they take us out for dinner at the DuPont Country Club, where they are members. They talk nonstop, but I am quiet as a lamb. I am afraid of humiliating myself, so I watch everything they do and follow their lead. I have never been to any place as elegant as the DuPont Country Club. The next day I have another new experience. We go to the DuPont Hotel for brunch. The closest experience I can think of is the Hotel St. George where St. Vincent's Home had their annual fund-raising dinner. I am completely impressed and feel completely out of place.

I think ruefully of my own upbringing. Bill and Mabel assure me that had they known of my existence they would have taken me from foster care and raised me as their own. Andy, too, makes it very clear that his parents would have done whatever they could to see that their nephew was not abandoned. I fantasize how they would have made my parents sign those papers releasing me for adoption,

DA's Sleuth Plays Father At Orphanage

Edward A. Rohs, 25, of 20 Plaza St., Park Slope, who grew up in St. Vincent Home for Boys, Boerum Place and Smith St., Brooklyn, spends most of his spare time being a friend and pal to the boys living there now.

Rohs, a detective investigator for District Attorney Eugene Gold for almost two years, works in the Criminal Courts Building at 120 Schermerhorn St., Brooklyn. He is assistant to the chief of the complaint room.

Rohs, who was graduated from New York City Community College, is studying education nights at St. Francis College. Eventually, he plans to teach.

"Since I was an orphan myself, I know what it feels like to need a friend," he said. "I know how necessary it is for people to take an interest in boys at the home."

Coaches Ball Teams

Rohs coaches basketball and baseball teams at St. Vincent. There are some 140 boys ranging from 9 to 18 at the home. They are orphans or come from broken homes.

He also takes groups of the boys on field trips to such spots as the Baseball Hall of Fame in Coopertown, Bear Mountain, and Howe Caverns upstate and to basketball and baseball games.

Also, during each summer Rohs passes three weeks coaching baseball at a camp in Lackawaxen, Pa.

"Occasionally, I run across a boy who lives in the home and has been arrested," he said.

"One of these recently was a boy who was arrested on a misdemeanor charge. He was very ashamed, and told me he was sorry about what had happened."

Gratitude

Rohs appealed to the judge before whom the lad's case came up, and asked for a conditional discharge for the boy, provided he entered a job corps program. The judge granted permission for this, and the boy entered a job corps program in Texas.

Before he left for Texas, the boy told his probation officer; "Do me a big favor, and thank Eddie Rohs for what he did for me."

Before going to work for the district attorney's office, Rohs worked as an administrative aide for the Police Department.

Ed A. Rohs

Uncle Bill finds me after reading this article. (New York Daily News, L.P. Used with permission.)

and how I would have been raised as Bob's or Andy's brother, experiencing all the pleasures of their life.

I ponder what would have happened if they discovered me when I was older. I know that the transition would have been difficult. But, in the end, it would have been OK, because whoever took me, and whenever they took me, I would have had the opportunity to experience what it meant to have family and to be loved.

11   Inventing Another New Life

I am twenty-six years old and on top of the world. I have a good job with the Brooklyn DA's office. For the first time in my life I am able to save money. I coach football, basketball, and baseball part-time at St. Vincent's Home. I live in a great apartment in a great neighborhood with a twenty-four-hour doorman. And I have a personal commendation from the president of the United States!

Then, one Friday evening in spring, 1972, it all comes crashing down. I come home from the DA's office to find a letter from personnel in my mailbox. Because of a severe fiscal crisis I have been terminated, effective immediately.

Nobody warned me that this was going to happen. The letter brusquely instructs me to report on the following Monday to turn in my gun and shield. With that letter, I lose more than my job. Two years earlier, I began taking evening classes at a community college with the aim of getting a college degree. After successfully completing thirty credits, I transferred to St. Francis College under the auspices of the federally sponsored Law Enforcement Assistance Program (LEAP), which encouraged local police department and other law enforcement employees to obtain their college degrees. I eventually transferred to Fordham University at Lincoln Center in Manhattan. I am proud of the progress I have made since my days as a marginal student at John Jay High School and am careful to toe the line. But now that I am no longer working for law enforcement I don't qualify for LEAP, and if I want to continue I will have to pay for college myself. I decide to put that dream on hold until I can figure out where I am going to be working.

Return to St. Vincent's

Word travels quickly, and out of nowhere I get a call from Henry J. Floyd, director of childcare workers at St. Vincent's Home. He began working at the home in the summer of 1965, after I had left, but we became friends after I began coaching the boys in my spare time. Henry offers me a job as a childcare worker.

I have mixed feelings about going back to work at the home. I know that the average person would probably say, "Here's a chance to save money on food and rent." But when you've lived in an institution for all of your formative years and you have to go back to that institution because you've lost your job, it represents far more than just new employment. I blame myself for losing the job. I see myself as a complete failure, and resurrect old feelings of insecurity. I am afraid I cannot cut the cord and achieve independence. In fact, a couple of former Vinnie Boys whom I have kept in touch with actively discourage me from going back. They are very blunt, saying things like, "What's your problem. Why can't you make it on your own and get hired to do a real job?" They hint that I lack the inner strength to break away from institutional living, and in some ways, deep inside, I am afraid there is some truth to what they are saying—that I am returning to the security blanket of the home.

I take the job. It is a very tough decision for me to make, but I take it because—well, I have to eat. It also means that I can continue going to Fordham University during the day.

It is June and school is letting out, so I am assigned to the summer camp where I had some of my happiest experiences as a kid. But things have changed. The federal government has exercised its right of eminent domain and purchased Camp Christopher to build a dam. The camp that I had known as a child ceased to exist, but

I return to a renovated and spruced-up St. Vincent's.

St. Vincent's has acquired a new Pennsylvania campsite on the Delaware and Lackawaxen Rivers. Camp St. Vincent's has everything a boys' summer camp should have, with the additional allure of being close to Pennsylvania's Zane Grey Museum, honoring the home of the popular adventure novelist. The new monsignor in charge has built a learning center, supervised by a teacher certified in special education; there is also a bus that transports some campers to and from Port Jervis High School, giving them the opportunity to make up subjects they may have failed during the year.

I sleep in a cabin with ten campers ages fifteen to seventeen from the institution, and with two summer camp counselors to assist me. One is a college student, and the other is a foreign exchange student, one of several that St. Vincent's hires from the American International Foreign Exchange. Working for Camp St. Vincent's, they have an opportunity to learn about black and Hispanic children in the United States. And in fact, because many of these exchange students come from European countries that have few blacks or Hispanics, it is a rewarding experience for both them and the campers, who are streetwise kids and eager to share their world with curious and open-minded people. And although I initially have reservations regarding how effective exchange students would be in getting the campers to respond to discipline and structure, they develop genuine trusting relationships with the boys.

Turf War

Soon after I arrive at the camp, I am dismayed to find that our neighbors, "the locals," have not been accepting of our camp because it is composed mostly of black and Hispanic children and black staff. I hear stories that the locals used to drive up and down the road in their pickup trucks in the middle of the night with shotguns trying to intimidate St. Vincent's into selling the camp and leaving. I am told that the camp was not hassled when it was a Jewish camp because "at least it was white," according to a caretaker, who is a transplant from Mississippi. But it is he, in fact, who later becomes a big player in getting the locals to accept Camp St. Vincent's as their new neighbors.

For their part, the St. Vincent's Home administration has no intention of being bullied into selling their property. They feel very strongly that the kids in the downtown Brooklyn institution need a place to go for a summer break. So the administration develops a comprehensive plan to build good community relations, adding economic incentives in the hope that we will be accepted as neighbors.

Camp personnel hires a local resident as caretaker and provides him with a rent-free home; and they also hire locals to work in the office and maintenance departments during the summer months. The locals can see with their own eyes that black and Hispanic adolescent boys are just kids and in no way live up to their reputation as troublemakers. Camp staff members are encouraged to open savings and checking accounts at the local bank. Finally, after work, the staff and camp counselors patronize the local bars and restaurants in the surrounding area. (Of course, there are some exceptions. It is not easy being black or Hispanic in Lackawaxen, and some places are judged too dangerous to be frequented.) The owner of the local pub, the Jungle Jim, which is located close to the nearby Zane Grey Museum, is also a state trooper. He is an excellent friend and mediator between Camp St. Vincent's and the local community, and is able to defuse many potentially scary situations. He is often invited to Camp St. Vincent's.

When summer ends I return to the city, where I become dorm counselor to twenty boys, ages fifteen to seventeen. It means going back to those same dormitories that I slept in, although now I have my own counselor room in the dormitory. I return to my apartment on Plaza Street on my days off. It is my getaway. In the end, my friends support the decision to work at the home, even though they do not agree.

Since 1965, when I left the institution, I am delighted to find that there have been many positive changes. For one, the food is a thousand times better than the swill I was forced to eat. Ebinger's mosh pit is gone, as are cafeteria-style slops and metal trays. Now there is a full-time dietitian and family-style meals with real plates and utensils, glassware, and even—hallelujah—second servings. And the kids do not have to select their clothes from wholesale distributors: they now can go out and do all their shopping on Fulton Street with purchase orders that store owners honor.

The residents still live in dormitories, but some dorms have been converted into rooms for four youngsters. At Christmastime the home is gaily decorated with Christmas trees and ornaments, and the kids no longer get their weekly laundry wrapped in Christmas paper as a holiday gift. Now they submit a wish list to Santa and every attempt is made to honor their requests. And instead of being identified by a number, the dorms were now named after Catholic bishops and former presidents of the United States. Dorm 1 is Ford Hall, Dorm 2 is Spellman Hall, Dorm 3 is Casey Hall, Dorm 4 is Blake

Hall, Dorm 5 is Independence Hall, Dorm 6, which houses young men who attend college, is named Lincoln Hall, Dorm 7 is Malloy Hall, and Dorm 8 is Kennedy Hall.

Residents are Protestant and Catholic, and services are offered for both denominations. The staff itself is of a higher caliber. Dorm counselors are now called childcare workers and do much more than custodial care. They are required to have a minimum of two years of college and to utilize behavior modification rather than punishment. Weekly allowances and pass privileges are now given as rewards, rather than being withheld to punish misbehavior. This is a drastic improvement from my day. Finally, because the kids coming in have spent less time in institutions and often come from abusive homes, there are more medical and clinical services available. There is no public address system. And thank goodness, reveille has been eliminated.

I find that the adolescents in placement are definitely more streetwise and have much better survival skills than I ever had when I was in care. The majority of them have come in through the local Family Court—that is, they are remanded by the court to St. Vincent's via the NYC Human Resources Administration Office of Special Services for Children (SSC). They enter care having experienced more social, emotional, physical, and psychological abuse then I ever experienced in my lifetime. Without downplaying their significance, my two isolated incidents of physical and sexual abuse at the hands of people who were supposed to protect me are peanuts when compared with the case records that I read describing the lives of these boys. They are more difficult to deal with than the kids I was raised with, as they are wilder and unaccustomed to institutional discipline.

But even though they need more discipline and structure than I ever did, I find that these children also need more understanding and support services to get them through the physical and psychological trauma they experienced from their biological parents or surrogates. I hear their stories and recognize that the scars I carry from childhood are nothing compared to the horrendous physical and emotional abuses these kids have encountered on a daily basis before they were removed from the care of their crack/alcohol/heroin–addicted or emotionally disturbed parents or guardians.

Although they are tougher psychologically than the kids I knew growing up, I enjoy working with them immensely because I take the approach that we have much to learn from one another. Though I am seen as a very strict disciplinarian who plays by the rules, I try to convey to them that I care about them as human beings. I try to teach them that at a certain point in life they must take ownership of their behavior and become productive citizens despite the obstacles they have had to overcome. When I use myself as an example and tell them that I lived in the same dormitories as they now live, their eyes widen in disbelief. Having lived in five institutions, going back to St. Vincent's Home to work as a dormitory counselor gives me the opportunity to see things from a counselor's perspective.

The Other Side

Now I am seeing what it is like to supervise eighteen to twenty adolescent boys in a dormitory all by myself, being responsible for waking them up when they do not want to get out of bed. I knew what it was like to be an unhappy kid. Now I see how hard it is to get groups of fifteen- to seventeen-year-olds to dress and make their beds, wash their faces, brush their teeth, comb their hair, put their school clothes on, do their dormitory chores, get down to breakfast on time, get their school transportation, and get them off to school. And the schedule that controlled my life as a kid is still in force. Only now I am looking at it from the other side.

At three o'clock I distribute afternoon snacks to the boys who have returned from school. I make sure they change from their school clothes into play clothes, and send them down to the recreation department or side yard to play or give them a pass to leave the building. At five o'clock I count heads to ensure that everyone is present and then herd them into the dining room for supper, where I monitor them to make sure they sit in their assigned seats during the meal. When they finish eating I make sure that all of them have cleaned their eating area and brought their dirty trays and dishes to the dishwasher. At seven o'clock I have to make sure all the boys sit around the table in the dormitory for two-hour study hall, seeing that kids who have tutors go down to see their them and that there is no horsing around. At nine o'clock the boys play for a half hour and then start preparing for bed, and I make sure they go from the fourth-floor dormitory to the basement to take their daily showers. At nine thirty I distribute bedtime snacks to those youngsters who are ready for bed. At ten o'clock I make sure all eighteen youngsters are in bed. My bedroom is in the dormitory. After they are all in bed I can take off for an hour and go around the corner to the store for myself. I am in bed by eleven thirty.

During the week I am a stern disciplinarian, but on the weekend I show my caring side. On Saturday mornings it is my treat! I go to the store and purchase half gallons of orange juice and donuts. With memories of being dragged from my bed too early on weekend mornings, I let the kids sleep until ten o'clock. My job is exhausting, and after doing it for seven months I develop a better appreciation and understanding of how hard the nuns, brothers, and laypeople worked in the dormitories during my formative years.

Eventually I am promoted from senior dorm counselor to child-care supervisor. But there is a downside because now that I am no longer a dorm counselor I do not work directly with the kids. They feel abandoned, and they respond by becoming totally uncooperative, going out of their way to ignore their new dorm counselor and making his job impossible. At first I don't realize what's happening, but after a month I get wind of it and decide to step down and go back to working in the dorm. But then Henry Floyd hears about the situation and calls an emergency dorm meeting to iron things out. In the end, I retain my position and the kids cut the new dorm counselor some slack.

A Bright Troublemaker Who Made Me Laugh

Gary is a very bright and troubled seventeen-year-old who attends Erasmus Hall High School. One day he is suspended for threatening a teacher. Marjorie Barnwell, the social work supervisor, and I meet with him to decide how to proceed. I start by asking if he knows why we were meeting, to which he responds, "Of course I understand. Do you think I'm an idiot?"

OK, so what is his side of the story? Very seriously he tells us the following: "I'm just sitting there and the teacher comes back to my desk and snatches my portable transistor radio right out of my hand. I can't let him do that to me, and I tell him, 'Listen, Teach, if you ever snatch a radio out of my hand again, I'll shove it so far up your butt you'll be spitting batteries out your mouth.' Mr. Rohs, it's not my fault the class started laughing. Next thing I know, the teacher yells out, 'Get out—out! You're suspended.'"

Marjorie and I excuse ourselves. We flee the room and try to keep our hysterical laughter down to a muted cackle. After we regain our composure and reenter the room, I tell him, "You're charmed. If it was me, Gary, I'd have suspended you for the entire year."

My Pride and My Fall

It is 1976 and I am almost finished with all the requirements for a bachelor's degree at Fordham. I am still living in my great apartment on Grand Army Plaza, I am proud of my rapid promotion to supervisor and the world looks good. Unfortunately, it goes to my head, and when I am not considered for promotion to unit director—well, I quit. I accept a supervisor position at another childcare institution, way up in Sparkill, New York. Boy, is that a mistake! Geographically, I am totally messed up. I live in Brooklyn, I go to college in Manhattan, but now I am working thirty miles upstate. Henry Floyd tries to convince me to think it through before I make a stupid decision, but I cannot listen to reason. In hindsight, I realize that I was not educationally or emotionally ready for the director's position, and that the people in charge had made a commitment to upgrade the quality of care by hiring staff with master's level credentials.

Tough Love

So I abruptly leave St. Vincent's Home for St. Agnes Home for Boys, operated by the Dominican Sisters in Sparkill. On my first day I am delighted to discover that the sisters have appointed their first lay executive director, Mr. Ralph Kelly, who had been one of my favorite childcare workers when I was an adolescent at St. Vincent's. My responsibility at St. Agnes is to supervise twelve adolescent boys with a staff of seven in a resident cottage.

 I work from three in the afternoon to eleven at night. I can continue my studies but the schedule is grueling: From my home in Brooklyn I take the IRT subway to Fordham's Lincoln Center campus at West 60th Street. After my classes at Fordham I jump on the subway at 59th down to 42nd Street, where I get off and race over to the Port Authority Bus Terminal. That is where I catch the two o'clock Short Line Bus to Sparkill, which, thankfully, lets me off right in front of St. Agnes. At eleven o'clock I leave the cottage and take the bus back to the city and get off at the 178th Street George Washington Bridge Bus Terminal, where I pick up the A train subway down to 59th Street. Then I catch the D train back to Brooklyn. I arrive at my home around one o'clock in the morning.

Memories of a Volkswagen

Sparkill is a beautiful place to work, but my schedule is killing me. I purchase a beat-up tan Volkswagen squareback, hoping it will reduce the stress of my commute. Driving, I shave off an hour and get home around midnight. I spend a couple of hours studying, and make it to class by 8:30 in the morning. I am starting to question if I made the right decision quitting my job at St. Vincent's Home, but I keep those doubts to myself. Somehow I will muddle through.

When St. Agnes announces that they are holding their annual Christmas Party at a local Sparkill restaurant, I invite a beautiful Hispanic nurse who works at Long Island College Hospital in Brooklyn. I had met her at another Christmas party a couple of weeks before, organized by the hospital's nursing department. I am elated. The Sparkill party will be a great first date!

The night of the party it is absolutely freezing. I pick her up in Manhattan and we have a nice ride up to Sparkill in my Volkswagen. We have fun and I am feeling fine. Driving home along the Palisades Parkway, I am handling the freezing rain and even the windshield wiper that shuts down on the passenger side. Then, out of nowhere, the heating pipe develops a glitch and suddenly the car becomes glacial. My date is shaking uncontrollably and I have to give her my own winter coat. I apologize to her a thousand times, but when I finally get her home I know it is over. She confirms my suspicions by not answering my telephone calls. Oh, that Volkswagen!

But my car is not through giving me grief. It is in the pre-computer, pre-photocopy days, and I remember typing an English term paper for a Professor Vaughan and proudly placing it next to the driver's seat in my Volkswagen when I went to work at St. Agnes. Psychologically, I think I needed to get it off my desk and on its way to the professor. But that is not what happened. Late that evening as I drive home with the window open, I watch in horror as the paper flies out the window. The next morning I present myself to the professor to explain what happened and beg my case for more time to rewrite the paper. Not surprisingly, she is short on sympathy and gives me a one-day extension. I get home from work at midnight and begin working on a new paper at 2:00 A.M. and into the next day. I am totally exhausted but determined, come what may, to submit that paper and complete the course.

On my way back to St. Agnes I see a cute little truck, named Little Patrol Truck, picking up garbage. I am desperate, so I stop the driver and ask if he remembers picking up any papers. To my surprise he says, "Be my guest," and points to the barrel of garbage on the back of the truck. I plow into it, inspecting each piece of paper. Lo and behold, I find my term paper, all wet and wrinkled, but intact.

The next day I arrive at Professor Vaughan's office and explain what happened. Then I hand her my paper, which by now is a soggy mess. Her eyes grow wide with amazement and she says, "Mr. Rohs, you have to understand something. During exam time students come to me with thousands of reasons why they can't submit their reports on time. You wouldn't believe the number of deaths of aunts, uncles, cousins—all occurring during exam week. Nonetheless, Mr. Rohs, I can't make a blanket judgment. I have to look at each case and make decisions based on each student as an individual. Mr. Rohs, your story just showed me that I need to trust my students."

Professor Vaughan gives me an A.

Surviving

I become irritable and find myself snapping at everyone—youngsters and staff alike. Clearly, I am burning out. Six months after arriving, and without another job lined up, I abruptly quit—yet another stupid decision. Over the next eight months I become financially desperate. Childcare agencies seldom return the calls I make because I now have a reputation for walking off the job and leaving supervisors in the lurch. I deplete my savings and subsist on juice and a bowl of cereal every morning, and bologna and American cheese on white bread for lunch and dinner. Sometimes all I have is a can of soup. Sometimes I go to bed hungry. I have too much pride to ask friends for assistance, although when I visit them on weekends—Henry Floyd and his wife, Lelar, in Flatbush, Harry and Aida Perez on Staten Island, or Aunt Katherine in Sunset Park—I eat like there is no tomorrow.

Somehow, I manage to keep up with my studies at Fordham, which makes me feel like less of a loser. I often stop by the Fordham career planning office to check out part-time jobs that may be available. On two occasions I find very brief employment as a security guard for a firm contracted by the Democratic National Convention held at Madison Square Garden. I am thirty years old and broke.

The year is 1976, and I am having no luck finding any type of employment except for those odd jobs I am getting from Fordham. I get a great temporary job working as a security guard at the New York Gift Show in the New York Coliseum. I am a conscientious worker and when the show ends my supervisor asks me to stay on with his skeleton crew to guard the merchandise while vendors pack up to go to the next big city. It is a Saturday, and I am marching up and down the hall, proud of the outstanding job I am doing keeping thieves from stealing goods. Then the supervisor comes around.

"How is it going, Ed Rohs?"

"There hasn't been any thievery on my watch."

He rolls his eyes at me and says, "Let me show you something."

He takes me around and starts pointing out all the hiding places where robbers have stashed stolen goods. I am embarrassed and humiliated, but he is a good guy and he tells me, "Ed, they knew you were new and wet behind the ears. They have a lookout guy with a full-time job of watching every move you made. They hit when you went to the bathroom. Most of these guys are honest but there's always a bad apple; you just didn't know." Of course, he has to let me go, but it is quite a learning experience.

I deal with my unemployment by jogging in Prospect Park. I am doing up to seven miles a day and it is the best therapy in the world. From this experience I learn an important lesson: Never quit a job until you have something else lined up. And after eight months of being unemployed, I deplete my life savings. I realize that I have made stupid decisions, using my heart and not my brain, and I know this definitely is something I have to work on. In fact, I make a commitment to myself that once I get back on my feet, I will never walk out of another job unless I have something else lined up.

I finally get an interview for a job at New York Foundling Hospital. I am desperate and at rock bottom, and I am so nervous that the night before my interview I cannot sleep. I dress up in my interview suit but discover I have only enough money to take a subway to the interview in Manhattan, but not enough to get me back home to Brooklyn.

I arrive at the interview thirty minutes early and complete the employment application. I am pretty confident that I can ace the interview because I have a great deal of knowledge about childcare and supervising staff. After we talk for awhile, the director tells me that he will be in touch. I thank him profusely for taking the time out from his busy schedule. I walk to the subway station on the Upper East Side of Manhattan, an upscale neighborhood, walk downstairs to the subway entrance, and remember I have no money. I am too embarrassed to ask the token booth clerk if I can go through the turnstile for free, so I stand around for fifteen minutes. Finally, I tell myself, *What the heck, I have nothing to lose.* I approach the token booth clerk and say, "Excuse me, I just came back from an interview for a job at the New York Foundling Hospital, but have no money to buy a token for the trip back home. Could you please let me go through the turnstile?" She snaps back, "No, talk to a cop."

"Please?"

"Didn't you hear me? I said talk to a police officer."

I am angry and humiliated, but I bite my tongue. Besides, there is no cop to be found. I am now working up enough nerve to panhandle and ask people coming down or going up from the subway for money. The first few people I ask give me this look like I am annoying them. I cannot believe I am panhandling, and I hope and pray that nobody from St. Vincent's Home or any other institutions I have been at sees me. I think about my former life in the DA's office and police department and I look with dismay at where I am today, begging for a subway token.

Through it all I try to keep my head up and not dig a hole and jump in. Finally, a lady gives me the coins to get my token. I thank her profusely, but she does not look like she really believes me. I think she just wants me to go away, which I am more than happy to do.

The subway panhandling is the most humiliating experience I have ever had in my life. But the fates have more in store for me. For the next couple of days I call the director at the hospital. At first, he answers my calls and seems friendly and supportive. I figure he is waiting for references because the job is supervising staff and kids, but no such luck. As the weeks go by, he stops returning my messages and his secretary sounds annoyed.

Welcome to Bushwick

Finally, after eight months, I land a job at a "hard-to-place" group home for adolescents in an area of Brooklyn I have never been—Bushwick. Before a boy can be admitted to this home he has to have been rejected by at least six other foster care agencies. That is why it is called "hard to place" by the NYC agency that funds it, Special Services for Children (now Administration for Children's Services). I am told that this institution, St. Christopher's Group Home, can't seem to keep its staff, and as soon as I arrive I know why. The neighborhood is completely burned out. But I find myself excited by the challenge of working with these kids and very happy to have a job again. My hours were usually 8:00 A.M. to 4:00 P.M., Monday through Friday, unless a staff member calls in sick. The home can't ever go uncovered by staff, and since staff work either 3:00 P.M. to 11:00 P.M. or 11:00 P.M. to 7:00 A.M., if I cannot get a staff member to cover and work overtime for either pay or compensatory time, as supervisor I'm the one who has to do the double shifts.

One night, as the kids are getting ready for bed, shooting starts down the block on the corner of Suydam Street and Central Avenue.

I stick my head out of a second-story window and begin screaming at the top of my lungs for everyone to keep their heads in and
away from the windows. I see the shooter plugging bullets into a guy
who is lying motionless on the sidewalk and appears already dead.
When he hears me scream from the window the shooter runs past
St. Christopher's home, stops, and looks up at me, his gun shining
under the streetlight. For an endless second I think, *I am dead.* When
the police arrive, they do not even bother to ask questions. It's as if
they're telling me, "Welcome to Bushwick, where shootings happen
every day."

During the blackout in 1977 Bushwick burns. Kids leave the
group home to go two blocks away to loot businesses that have been
burned out. They are upset when they return and find me standing
in the doorway, arms out, blocking them from bringing stolen merchandise into the building—clothes, stereo equipment, lamps, boom
boxes—you name it, they have it. They beg me to let them in with
their booty. But by then I have learned that if I am firm and consistent, and if I show that I really love working with them, these kids
will respond. Amid the mayhem, I feel it is important for me to be a
positive role model.

The morning after the blackout I take a group of youngsters on a
tour of what is left of the community. We drive our twelve-passenger
van to Broadway in East New York, Brooklyn, which is three blocks
away from our group home. Even in the morning the stores are being vandalized. People approach our van, trying to sell the goods
they have looted the night before. Most of the merchandise comes
from stores that are owned predominantly by Jews. Then we drive in
the opposite direction, over to Knickerbocker Avenue. These stores
are predominantly Italian American owned, and not one store is
damaged. As we drive by, I cannot help but notice that there are cars
and trucks parked on the sidewalks right in front of the stores, with
owners inside holding shotguns, protecting their property. It feels
like something out of the Wild West. I point it out to the kids, and

we cannot believe the contrast between the two communities. One community has been burned out and the other appears untouched.

Protection

Late one night as I return from work, I bump into a gang chasing someone down the stairs of the subway station with knives, chains, and bats. They stop for a second to look at me. My heart is in my throat, but then they turn and continue chasing the other guy.

I am the only white person in the community but they leave me alone. It is not the first time. I ask the streetwise youngsters I work with why I do not get attacked. They tell me that "the whole neighborhood knows you work with us hoodlums. Anybody that works with us must be tough—or nuts. Either way they don't want to touch you." I am very happy to have acquired this reputation.

Unfortunately, it does not prevent my kids from stealing from the home. I remember picking up toiletries for the kids at the group home from the main campus in Sea Cliff out on Long Island. I bring them back and secure them in a storage facility in the basement. Over the weekend I get a call from the police at the 83rd Precinct to report that they have a couple of my kids locked up. I arrive at the precinct and I see the two youngsters. I ask what they stole and I am shown my barrel of toiletries. I am so ticked off that I turn to the cops and announce, "Keep 'em locked up. I'll see them in arraignment." The two seventeen-year-old kids are in total shock that I won't agree to let the police officer release them to me. It's just my way of letting everyone at St. Christopher's get the message that I am not going to tolerate anyone stealing our supplies and selling them on the street. On Monday I meet them in court and the judge releases them to me.

And then there is Napoleon Bonaparte. At six feet three inches, Napoleon does pretty much what he wants, and what he wants is to steal stuff from the group home and sell it to the local bodega. All his friends are getting fed up because, in a sense, he is stealing from them. Every time I make a purchase he steals it, and I do not mean cans of soup: this kid walks off with furniture, toasters, end tables, lamps. I tell him, "Bonaparte, one day I'm gonna catch you, and then you're going to catch hell."

Eventually I get a call from the kids themselves to report that Bonaparte just stole a toaster and he has already sold it to the bodega. I tell the staff to keep him in the home. I go to the bodega and there, at the end of the counter, is the brand-new toaster. I say to the owner, "It's my toaster. Tell me who sold you my toaster." The shopkeeper is terrified, and he does not speak much English anyway. I ask him again—and again—"Who is he?" Finally, just as he looks about to speak, in walks Bonaparte, glaring menacingly at him. The guy shuts up and I don't get my toaster. But after this experience, Napoleon Bonaparte feels the heat and leaves the group home stuff alone.

Overall, thefts in that group home went down dramatically after they got the message that the punishment I would inflict for stealing our stuff made it too much of a hassle.

12   **Milestones**

In 1978 I graduate from Fordham University with a Bachelor of Arts degree in social science and am accepted at the Fordham's Graduate School of Social Service. I am thirty-one years old, and a party is held in my honor. It is the first time that anyone has made a party just for me. My cousin Andy makes the arrangements, and among the guests are the members of my self-made family: Aunt Katherine, Sister Johanna, Harry and Aida Perez, and Henry and Lelar Floyd. I feel empowered, but I have learned my lesson about leaving jobs too quickly, and I remain at St. Christopher's until after my graduation.

Lelar, who is director of social work at Lutheran Community Services, hires me as a social worker for their two group homes in the Bronx, one for boys and one for girls, and allows me to work ten-hour days, four days a week, so I can attend graduate school on the fifth day. I work at Lutheran for one year, but when I enter my second year of graduate work I must leave that agency because Fordham requires that second-year graduate students work in the school's field placements and that we not hold down a full-time job.

I get a very good field placement interning for Dr. Katherine White, who is the executive director of the Catholic Child Care Society (later renamed HeartShare). I remember her telling me, "You can have all the interviewing skills in the world, but when everything else fails, always go with your gut."

The Catholic Child Care Society pays me a small stipend, and in addition, to make ends meet, I find a weekend job with a Methodist church, where I am responsible for cleaning their grounds, the church itself, and their school. In the spring of 1980, I receive my master's degree in social work, and again, my cousin Andy coordinates a party to celebrate another milestone, this time at Lüchow's, New York's legendary German restaurant.

Now, degree in hand, I quit my weekend church job and return to St. Vincent's, where Henry Floyd hires me as camp recreation director. In this capacity I develop a ten-week recreation program for more than 140 campers, ages thirteen to eighteen, that starts at eight thirty in the morning and takes them through the day until lights out at nine thirty at night. It is both challenging and rewarding. For those ten weeks I work very, very hard, from 8:00 A.M. to 10:00 P.M., five days a week. But although the job is extremely demanding and I am completely exhausted at the end of the day, it is very rewarding to see these tough young men having a great time away from their urban stress. Coming from that world myself, I understand that for many kids their summer camp experience will be the best days of their lives. I know they will always remember Camp St. Vincent's. When the summer ends, I return to St. Vincent's in Brooklyn in a position equivalent to that of a unit director.

Ed Rohs, Camp Director

The following summer Henry promotes me to camp director, and it turns out to be the most demanding job I have ever had in my entire life. Even though I appreciate the confidence Henry has in me, and even though I think I understand the enormous responsibility of this assignment, I do not really have a full appreciation what is involved until I walk into the job. As the camp director, I am responsible for everything imaginable. Suddenly, everybody is coming to me for every little thing. I am completely new at handling these kinds of responsibilities (budget, payroll, staff, food service, maintenance, supervising assistant directors, supervisors, etc.); suddenly, I am the answer man. I realize that for many staff members it becomes easy for them to ask me, "What should I do with this? How should I handle this situation? How come I'm assigned to do this?" The most common questions are "What do you think?" and "How should I do this?" I notice that most people want to be given answers rather than to work out the answers for themselves.

I drive myself crazy trying to be the answer man. Eventually it dawns on me that I don't have to have all the answers, and I am able to tell people to return to their respective supervisors for assistance and direction. This valuable experience teaches me that it is easier to criticize and complain than it is to come up with solutions. I begin making rounds of the camp three times a day. Walking around, observing, and talking to campers and staff gives me a good feel for what is happening. I love walking about the campground, and I am able to do this because I have an excellent office staff and a particularly fine office manager, Ms. Francis. She is meticulous when it comes to details, and that frees me up to do my job in the field.

Recently, I asked Henry Floyd why he chose to appoint me as camp director. He said, "I knew you were a hard worker, very competitive, and insecure. And because of your insecurity coming from all the years you were raised in institutions, I knew you would want to prove you could do the job. You also had an MSW, and I thought you would be a very good role model for these kids. And maybe most importantly, I trusted you, and I was right, because you did a great job supervising sixty staff and one hundred and forty campers and working sixteen hours a day. Ed, they were the good days."

Being a camp director can be very stressful, entailing much time and commitment, but I like to think I was successful not only because I had the backing of Henry Floyd and the monsignor who ran St. Vincent's Home, Father Harris, but also because I gained the respect of both staff and campers. Nonetheless, I tried never to forget that some of the campers were emotionally disturbed and severely damaged youngsters. Two frightening, nightmarish incidents stick in my mind:

A youngster chases a staff member with a machete. The guy being chased is running for dear life across the campgrounds. There is no doubt that if he is caught by the kid he will be hacked to death. We chase the youngster, catch him, and tackle him to the ground. The machete is confiscated and the state police come and have the boy hospitalized.

Another time, a youngster constantly needles a camper who is much stronger but developmentally disabled. On several occasions I must admonish the teaser to knock it off. I warn him that one day the victim is going to lose his temper. Sure enough, one day while the entire camp is eating lunch in the dining room the strong kid is teased in front of his friends. He gets out of his chair, walks into the kitchen to the large coffee urn, and fills it with boiling water. Then he goes out to the table of the tormentor and throws the scorching water in his face.

We rush the boy who has been burnt to the camp infirmary and then to the hospital, where he is treated for third-degree burns. The attacker is escorted from the dining room to the camp administrative offices. Besides being counseled by the administrative staff, his social worker and treating psychiatrist are contacted. They decide that he is not a danger to himself or other campers and staff, but he receives ongoing counseling. There are no further incidents. Fortunately, the boys don't share a dorm and after the attack, staff members watch these two young men very, very carefully!

Laurence Preacher

The major difference between Camp Christopher and Camp St. Vincent's is that St. Vincent's has a swimming pool. The convergence of the Delaware and Lackawaxen rivers creates dangerous currents, so swimming in the river is strictly forbidden. One afternoon, two staff members take their ten cabin charges on a hike along the Delaware River. Three campers venture into the river to cool off, but they do not know how to swim and the current is fierce. Two are able to fight their way to shore, but Laurence Preacher, one of the camp counselors, spots the third boy as he is being dragged under. Laurence jumps into the river to rescue the boy and succeeds in saving his life, but in the process he is dragged down himself and drowns.

The other campers and staff run back to the camp to report the horrible accident. I immediately notify the police, Henry Floyd, and Monsignor Harris. They and other staff members drive out to provide support. I feel helpless with shock and grief, but I am the camp director and I struggle to project a calm and serene facade. Even though I had warned everyone a thousand times not to venture into the river, I somehow blame myself. If only I had forbidden this hike. If only I had warned them one more time. If only . . .

The hardest part is meeting youngsters and staff in small groups to break the news, after which the entire 140 campers and staff come together to pray. On this day not one behavior problem is reported.

The following Wednesday I drive ninety miles down to Brooklyn as a representative of St. Vincent's to attend his wake and funeral service and to provide whatever comfort I can to his family. They bear the burden with enormous grace and dignity. The floral arrangement arrives from St. Vincent's, but there is nothing anyone can do to bring back this wonderful human being. I am heartbroken when I realize that even in the manner of his death, Lawrence Preacher remained a superb role model for boys.

I will never forget how frightened I was—and lonely. From that tragedy I developed a deeper understanding of the enormous burden leaders carry when, at the end of the day, responsibility rests on their shoulders alone.

Ed Rohs, Weight Training Coach

Between September 1981 and August 1982 I worked in Brooklyn as St. Vincent's recreation director. Then, in the summer of 1982, the

St. Vincent's board announces that it will close the institutional part of the agency while retaining the foster boarding home, group homes, and mental health services. Although I know it is a sound decision, since we cannot take proper care of these youngsters in such a large setting, I have a hard time watching the demise of the institution, which has been in existence for more than a hundred years. But times have changed, and by 1982 the "answer" to raising parentless, abandoned, or abused kids has shifted from institutionalization to foster care.

Once again I am unemployed, but now I am a certified social worker and so have more confidence in my employment opportunities. I make a decision not to rush into a job and to take advantage of Fordham University's Rose Hill Campus in the Bronx, which is known for its outstanding athletic and recreational facility. From June to September I work out in the weight room, getting in top condition both physically and emotionally. It is during this time that I develop an excellent relationship with two of the Division I NCAA varsity basketball players, Steven Samuels and James Robinson.

When I start volunteering in 1982, most universities and colleges in the country do not have formalized weight training programs for basketball players. But I realize that these young men are looking for guidance and instruction on how to get big and strong, and that I had better start learning the basic principles of weight training so I can be a real asset. This means doing research on weight training and conditioning at the Fordham University library and reviewing NCAA material on effective methods of training. I help these players with weight training and conditioning, and eventually I volunteer my services as strength coach for the entire basketball team. At the time, coaches feared that weight training would negatively affect their players' flexibility and agility on the basketball court, and they frowned on kids going to the weight room. It is to the credit of Head Coach Tom Penders that once he sees James and Steven improve their performance, he gives me my start as a volunteer strength and conditioning coach. After he leaves Fordham to become head coach at the University of Rhode Island, I have the chance to work with

A Standing Ovation

It is halftime on Alumni Day and naturally the game is completely sold out. At the start of the ceremonies honoring former Fordham basketball players, Coach Tom Pecora spends almost a full minute paying tribute to my twenty years as a volunteer strength coach and my ongoing connection with many former players. I later find out that this is the first time in more than a hundred years that a Fordham coach has publicly recognized a non-player on Alumni Day. I receive a standing ovation.

The only problem is that I am not around when it happens, because the Fordham basketball great Bevon Robin has asked me to take his eight-year-old daughter, Taylor, to a concession stand to buy her a hot dog, potato chips, and water while he lines up with other former players. So I am waiting on the long concession line with Taylor when, over the PA system, I hear, "Ed Rohs did . . . Ed Rohs is . . ." And then I see everyone stand up and start clapping and hooting and hollering to register appreciation for my years of service—except they cannot find me. When I finally return to my seat with Taylor, the people leading the ceremony start yelling, "Here he is, here he is" as the former players being honored give me high fives.

Coaches Bob Quinn and Nick Macarchuk, and each coach makes me part of the Fordham basketball family. In addition to weight training, I am able to utilize my social work skills to help student athletes develop their maximum potential. I am much more than a strength coach to these talented and gifted student-athletes. Despite their impressive physical size and talent, and although they have achieved a major victory by obtaining a full-time athletic scholarship to play Division I basketball, these young men have the same emotional needs as any college kid. The major difference is that their performance is always being scrutinized.

I worked with these athletes for seventeen years, and during that time the weight room became a place where they could talk to me in confidence about any problems they might be having. Although at times it was emotionally draining, I always demanded a lot, pushing and motivating them to give their absolute best. I tried to convey to them that if you do everything with passion and hard work, and if you believe in yourself, you can achieve anything you want. Today, they are part of my extended family.

On the Road

I have heard people say that college coaches just care about winning. But the coaches I worked with at Fordham were good role models who helped their players expand their horizons by providing them with well-rounded experiences. I remember staff meetings where Coach Nick Macarchuk spent time planning non-basketball activities. I heard Coaches Tom Penders and Bob Quinn ask staff members tasked with coordinating the road trip to research activities in the city we would be going to so the team did not sit in the room watching television when they were not working. They made sure the kids all stayed in decent hotels and had meals in good restaurants—and not just when they were having training meals. And they insisted that the players dress appropriately.

Because I was a respected weight training coach, both the players and the coaches assumed that I was at ease in social situations, and this became problematic when we were on the road. Although everyone understood that some students might be intimidated by hotels and fancy restaurants, the coaches took for granted that I was more sophisticated and worldly; they assumed that I knew how to order from a menu, that I could properly hold eating utensils, and that I understood how to tip the wait staff. Surely I knew how to deal with bellboys. Of course I knew all about room service and wake-up calls. They saw me as an educated adult male. What they did not understand was that I had led a very sheltered life. I did a good job of concealing my ignorance, but it took a long time before I was able to confidently negotiate the tricky landscape of polite society. In many ways, I was probably on the same level as the kids. What the coaches did not know was that as they taught the athletes to be comfortable in public situations, they were also teaching me.

When Tom Penders, Bob Quinn, and Nick Macarchuk invited me to work with their players in the weight room, I think they realized that I did not just see these student-athletes as basketball players. Rather, I saw them as young men with personal issues that sometimes negatively affected their performance, both in the classroom and on the court. As a trained clinical social worker, I had the expertise to help them grow emotionally and physically. When one of the coaches told me that he was afraid I might make his players weak, I had to explain to him that in the weight room I could develop both mind and body. And because they trusted and respected me, and because they saw see me as a mentor and positive role model, players started sharing personal and confidential issues that definitely could have a negative impact on their basketball performance. I used motivational and positive reinforcement skills to increase their confidence and self-esteem.

One dramatic event puts my relationship with these young men in perspective. I usually had weight training on Tuesdays, Thursdays, and Sundays. One Thursday evening, as soon as I walk into the weight room, one of the seniors on the basketball team comes running over and says with some urgency, "Ed, you have to talk to J. B. He has his duffel bag and he's about to just quit school and the team, give up his whole scholarship, and take the train back home. Hurry, he's right next door. He's about to start heading off campus for the train." And I see this big, hulking player with his duffel bag over his shoulder walking in from next door. I ask him where he is going with the bag. His immediate response is, "Ed, I'm quitting. I can't take it anymore. I've had it. This is too much pressure: basketball, school, the coaches . . . "

I spend the next hour using everything I have—my personal relationship with him and my clinical social work skills—to talk him through his panic. I can say with satisfaction that he remained on the team and graduated from Fordham three years later.

Although I have many extraordinary memories from my seventeen-year career, I especially cherish two events. The first occurred in the 1982–83 season, when Fordham won the Metro Atlantic Conference with a 54–53 victory over Iona in the title game at the New Jersey Meadowlands. It was my first year working for Tom Penders, and at that game I actually sat right behind the Fordham basketball basket when Mark Murphy hit the buzzer-beating shot. That year the team came quite close to making the NCAA March Madness Tournament, but because the MAC was a newly formed league they did not

The Fox

Whenever the team is on the road, the coach assigns Jim Wilson and me to room together. Jim, who is in charge of sports medicine, had a career as a standout baseball player in college and then the minor leagues.

Jim is married with two grown children and is affectionately known as "The Fox" by the team. He is a father figure to everyone and probably one of the most respected people I have ever met. He takes his job very seriously and has a way of making an injured athlete feel at ease. But equally impressive is his ability to have fun. Whether we are on the bus, the plane, the train, or in a hotel, the Fox has more one-liners than a late-night comedian. Over the course of ten wonderful years and as roommates in hundreds of hotels, we develop a wonderful rapport. The Fox sure knows how to tickle my funny bone so that I laugh out loud.

Fordham Basketball Team: Coaches-Players-Friends

Howie Evans—Former assistant coach, Fordham University

John Fitzpatrick—Former assistant coach, Fordham University

Paul Hewitt—Head coach, George Mason University and Georgia Tech; assistant coach, Fordham University

Nick Macarchuk—Former head coach, Fordham University

Tom Parrotta—Head coach, Canisius College; former player at Fordham University

Tom Penders—Former head coach, University of Houston, University of Texas, George Washington University, University of Rhode Island, Fordham University, Columbia University, and Tufts University

Jean Prioleau—Assistant coach, University of Colorado; former player at Fordham University

Fred Quartlebaum—Former assistant coach, University of Notre Dame, University of North Carolina, Iowa State University, and St. John's University; former player at Fordham University

Bob Quinn—Former head coach, Fordham University

Mike Rice—Head coach, Rutgers University; former player at Fordham University.

Edgar Della Rosa—Assistant coach, Manhattan College; former assistant coach, Fordham University

Frank Williams—Head coach, Oakland High School; former player at Fordham University

Jim Wilson (The Fox)—Former head trainer, Fordham University

get an automatic bid. Then, in the 1991–92 season, when the team moved from the Metro Atlantic Conference to the Patriot League, under coach Nick Macarchuk, Fordham became league champions after beating Holy Cross in overtime and made it to the NCAA Tournament for the second time since 1972.

Over the years, I traveled all over the country as part of the coaching staff and developed lifelong friendships with players and coaches. Some of these coaches are now nationally recognized. I am proud of having been part of an elite group that includes players, student managers, radio announcers, newspaper reporters, trainers, and sports physicians.

Psychotherapist and Counselor

After I receive my certification as a licensed social worker to provide psychotherapy to children and families, Felix Ruiz, who is a colleague of a former Vinnie Boy, recommends me for a part-time evening job as a psychotherapist at a mental health clinic in East New York, Brooklyn. It is an opportunity that I cannot resist. I am hired, and under supervision of the clinical director, the psychiatrist Benjamin Chu, I work several days a week and on Saturday mornings providing individual psychotherapy and counseling to children and adults. I am employed on a fee-for-service basis, which means I am paid only if the client shows up for the forty-five-minute session. But besides the pay and the pleasure I derive from helping people, I am learning a whole new profession and there is great potential for growth. For a while, going from the classroom to everyday practice is exciting, but in time I begin to feel limited in my work as a psychotherapist, because in that capacity I am able to help only those people on my caseload.

Meanwhile, I work full-time at Special Services for Children. For two and a half years, I review the case records of children in foster care agencies, as well as their policy and procedural manuals in New York City and the greater metropolitan area. I interview administrative and line staff and, of course, the children themselves. I have trouble believing that I have reached this milestone in my life, and that I am in a position to improve the quality of care for children placed in foster homes.

For the following two and a half years I inspect agencies contracted to prevent children from ending up in foster care by offering services to keep the family intact and the children at home. I see that when you bring the services to the homes of overwhelmed families, it can enable the child to remain at home. I see this as cutting-edge, because like my own personal family situation, perhaps if my parents had had in-home services they would have been able to keep me. At the same time, I also work with a group of dedicated individuals who are committed to seeing that children who were in foster care receive quality treatment. I enjoy learning about the business end of childcare and get hands-on experience about how oversight and monitoring with regulatory clout can effect change.

I am elated by the opportunity my job presents. I was raised in the system; then I spent years working directly with children in the system; and now I am part of a team that evaluates agencies in the system. Unlike the current system, there were limited resources during my years growing up in institutions, and the focus was primarily on control, discipline, and custodial care. There were no therapeutic or independent living skills provided, and in fact, I have no firsthand knowledge if there was an oversight and monitoring governmental agency in existence at that time. I see firsthand that when I go out and provide competent evaluation for agencies, I am positively affecting thousands of children. What an awesome experience it is for me!

New Challenges

In time I outgrow SSC and begin looking for other challenges. A former childcare worker with whom I worked at St. Vincent's Home is now an influential person on the New York City Health and Hospital Corporation (HHC) board of directors, which oversees the eleven public hospitals of New York City. Over the years, through my contacts in the weight room, I had been sending graduates of Fordham for summer and full-time employment to his community agency in the East

Tremont section of the Bronx. One day he slams his fist on his desk and screams at me, "When is Ed Rohs going to take care of Ed Rohs and not everybody else?" And with that he arranges an interview with the vice president for mental health at HHC. Six months after the interview I am hired as a senior program-planning specialist, which comes with a substantial salary increase. Other than my experience as a part-time psychotherapist, the mental health field is totally new to me.

Initially I am on probation, and to be honest, I have difficulty making the transition to this new arena. My immediate supervisor hints that my job may be in jeopardy, but being a seasoned supervisor and director by now, I know what needs to be done to rectify the situation. At our supervisory meetings I take down detailed notes of her specific concerns, and after the meeting I drop everything and give these issues priority. The supervisor is pleased and I pass my probation period. My primary responsibility is liaising with the eleven acute-care HHC public psychiatric emergency rooms, and I deal mostly with overcrowding issues. The second responsibility is liaising with the Harlem and Metropolitan Hospitals' Departments of Psychiatry. Most of the concerns at the hospitals are about transfer issues because of overcrowding, which is a chronic problem in public hospitals because this is where the working poor, the uninsured, and the impoverished go for care.

When I go from my comfort zone of child welfare into this new world of mental health, I am petrified. But I do not dare convey this to anybody in the new workplace. I am intimidated by HHC, which is the largest public health system in the United States. Conducting oversight and monitoring activities on behalf of what is now known as the Office of Behavioral Health is scary, and I assume a facade to conceal my lack of experience. In hindsight, however, I am convinced that these seasoned Department of Psychiatry administrators saw my fear a mile away. Shortly after beginning these oversight visits, I realize that these managerial oversight skills are universal and can be applied anywhere. I develop the expertise and confidence to do my job representing HHC. I walk with my head held high.

My role at HHC brings me into close contact with the leadership of other governmental mental health agencies and departments at both the state and local level through intergovernmental meetings.

I am at HHC from 1987 to 1994. Then I meet Nitza Mongelles, an assistant commissioner for the borough of Manhattan at the New York City Department of Mental Health, and she offers me a job as senior program-planning analyst in her office. The primary responsibility is overseeing and monitoring contracts and conducting annual program audits. This is right up my alley. And with rumors running rampant that HHC is planning layoffs in the central office, and with flashbacks of the 1972 layoffs in my mind, I make my decision to accept a job with the city.

The best feature of this new job is that I review all the community-based mental health providers and acute-care hospitals in Manhattan. In time I am promoted to Manhattan borough coordinator. In this role I supervise staff and am responsible for the assignment of program audits. I am also responsible for investigating complaints from consumers and mental health providers. Three years later I accept a similar position at the New York State Office of Mental Health, where I remain to this day.

Talk about a small world! It turns out that the new director of adult services is Joe Reilly, a person I worked with briefly at St. Agnes Home in Sparkill twenty-one years ago. I think that Joe is a godsend. And then he tells me that the reason why I have been appointed is that Linda Rosenberg, a former senior associate commissioner for the New York State Office of Mental Health, has approved it. She never forgot that several years earlier I was chairing a city-state meeting on getting access to state psychiatric beds for patients being discharged from local acute-care hospitals. Linda told Joe Reilly that she signed off because during that whole process I was a very fair person. Today she is president and CEO of the National Association for Behavioral Health, a powerful advocacy and lobbying association. And OMH Director Anita Appel continues the great tradition of quality mental health services for NYS residents.

Given my history, I find that my biggest challenge is maintaining my objectivity. I work hard—and I believe I succeed—in following to the letter the evaluation instruments I am given. I try to not bring my own biases into the room with me. Whether interviewing administrators, supervisors, line staff, or the children in care, I try to be consistent, looking at the specific standard that is required for a foster care agency to pass; evaluating whether there is documentation (in the case record or elsewhere); and interviewing agency personnel. At the end of the day, my goal is to ensure that the children they oversee receive quality care.

Once some of our New York State–licensed mental health housing agencies learn of my institutional upbringing, I start being invited to present at community residences and other housing meetings. These agencies include Federation Employment and Guidance Services (one of the largest social service organizations in the United States), The Bridge, Institute for Community Living, Urban Pathways, Bowery Residence Committee, OHEL, Pesach Tikvah–Hope Development, Services for the Under Served, and Transitional Living Services. A common thread runs through all these agencies: similar to my own experiences, they had recipients/consumers/residents who are afraid to move on to more independent living. Also, our agency—being the licensing, oversight, monitoring, and regulatory authority for the state, in partnership with our providers—believed that part of the path to personal rehabilitation and recovery for persons with behavioral health issues included living in independent housing. In fact, to back up this belief, our agency has been funding unlicensed, supported housing apartments to help consumers live independently.

The target populations for my presentations were people diagnosed with bipolar disorder, major depression, schizophrenia, and other mental health disorders. They were men and women, ranging in age from eighteen to seventy-five. The number of people in attendance could be anywhere between fifteen and a hundred. The receptions I received varied, from outright anger and hostility (this is the guy the agency sent to get us kicked out) to being very receptive. In fact, on one occasion, when a couple of staff came to one of my presentations, they feared that I was going to be attacked physically by a man whom I had apparently upset. But I knew otherwise because of my experience. I didn't internalize what the individual was saying when he pointed his finger in my face. He was just angry because I was suggesting that he should move on to more independent housing. In fact, the more he spoke the more it seemed to me that he was ready to move.

Before my motivational presentation, I do some preliminary work with the administrator in order to know my target audience: demographics, age, gender, ethnicity, diagnosis, length of stay in the community residence, where they are before admission, and so forth. When I am introduced to the community residents as "Mr. Rohs from the New York State Office of Mental Health," the room becomes completely silent. To relax the residents and set the stage for them to listen and become involved in the discussion, I try as much as possible to ask open-ended questions so they cannot get away with shaking their heads yes or no.

"Why does everybody think I'm here?" Most of the time, the responses will be, "To help us with discharge."

"By a show of hands, how many people have been living at this residence for five, ten, or fifteen years?"

"By a show of hands, how many people can take care of their rooms properly?"

"By a show of hands, how many people can take their medications on their own?"

"By a show of hands, how many people think they can do a little food shopping and cook a small meal for themselves?"

"By a show of hands, how many people think they can pay— either out of PA, SSI, or other income—thirty percent of their income toward their monthly rent?"

By the last question and show of hands, I can tell that there is less apprehension as to why I am visiting the residence or community meeting. And I can see that the staff in attendance are amazed at how I am able to lessen the residents' fears and set the stage for my presentation. But the last thing I say before beginning the presentation is, "All of you who raised your hands to all of the questions I've asked, you're telling me that you meet the criteria to live in one of our supported apartments. Therefore, because you've met the basic requirements to be admitted into an independent housing apartment, we have to explore what is preventing you from moving on."

And then I always say, "If I, Ed Rohs, can make it on my own after being raised in institutions for nineteen years, then any of you that answered all the questions can try and make that first step and ask your case manager for an application to be accepted and admitted into the supported housing."

I can see in their eyes that I have their full attention. I ask them if anybody had ever lived in a New York City homeless shelter or a local or state psychiatric center. I tell them that these kinds of facilities reminded me of my upbringing, with dozens of beds lined up in barrack-like quarters. My presentations never take more than thirty minutes. I count success based on the number of residents who subsequently go to their case managers or social workers and ask to complete the application for independent housing. I follow up several months later, and it is always heartening to hear that many long-term residents who attended my presentation are moving on to more independent housing.

My success in this arena helps me gain the experience and confidence to do motivational speeches at a variety of other forums, such as sports teams on both the high school and college levels.

In Paradise

I used to think that weekend getaways and summer homes were for rich people, but in 1990 Harry Perez and I each paid $6,000 for adjacent campground sites on Lake Adventure in Milford, Pennsylvania. We later purchased recreational campground vehicles, too.

Harry and I are on cloud nine. Just imagine! For less than $20,000 per unit, each of us owns a getaway in beautiful Pike County, north of the Pocono Mountains resort area. Lake Adventure has all the amenities a person would want in a vacation spot. We enjoy the lake, pool, clubhouse, playground for kids, basketball court, softball field, volleyball court, bocce area, fishing, boating, and a bunch of other recreational activities. We feel like rich gentlemen, but our dues are modest and cover all the necessities. Given my history, it is not surprising that initially I am uncomfortable coming to a family campground community, and that for the first couple of years I feel completely out of place. Eventually, after I go out there every weekend during the spring, summer, and fall and get to know the wonderful people who belong, I grow to love the experience.

Everyone at Lake Adventure is open and helpful, and I become involved in many activities. I volunteer to organize three-on-three basketball for teens every Sunday during the summer months. On any given Sunday, between six to eighteen adolescent boys and girls participate. I learn that all kids are the same—whether they come from institutions, group homes, or traditional family units. Treat kids with respect and they return the confidence tenfold.

In 2000 I run for the Lake Adventure board of directors. I lose the election twice, but before my third try someone who knows his way around Lake Adventure politics lets me know that the reason I keep losing is because the board president thinks that the people who back me are contentious. The president believes that if I am elected I will ally with them against him, so he uses his authority to convince voters to keep me off the board. I am advised to align myself with issues that are dear to the property-owning voters and to volunteer on several community committees so that I am known throughout this large community of more than 1,700 people.

Taking his advice, I volunteer to serve on the security committee, and lo and behold, at one meeting a temporary community manager trips up and distributes a confidential report revealing that an alarming number of people owe thousands of dollars in back dues to the community. In the spring of 2003 I make the back dues issue the focus of my nomination and I finally win.

When I lost in past elections I would see the board president wink at the winners. But now that I have won my first three-year term, I can tell he is not a happy man, even though he comes over and gives me a congratulatory handshake. The bottom line is that he wants people on the board whom he can control. He knows I am not that man. Following my election to the board, the chairman takes to harassing me and saying things to get my goat. He knows I have the support of the Lake Adventure swim team because I often volunteer as a timer at swim meets. So during a lunch break at a board meeting he comes up to me and, standing close to my face, says, "The swim team is full of s--t and I don't care who the f--k tells them."

Up until now he has only seen my polite, well-mannered side, but now he has tipped his hand and I see him for the immature bully he really is; being a big, strapping man, he uses intimidation and fear to get his way. So we are on brink and I have just about had it with him. So I say, "Let's clear this up in private," and direct him to the community manager's office. When he enters the room, for effect I slide the door behind me and go right up into his face, force eye contact, nose to nose, and shout, "What's your problem? I don't care how powerful you think you are. If you keep this up I'll treat you like s--t every time I see you." He responds, "I don't like you using the dues issues to get elected." Our interaction ends in a stalemate, with each of us glowering. But from that day forward he treats me with the utmost respect. Equally important, by standing up to him I win the respect of the board.

I Have a Near-Death Experience

The second Lake Adventure board meeting is called in June 2003, but I am vacationing at a new condo I recently purchased in Daytona Beach that I anticipate will become my primary residence when I decide it is time to retire. I have just been elected and believe it to be very bad form to miss the meeting, especially after the battles I have had to fight to get elected. So at seven in the morning on the day before the meeting I start driving up from my Florida home to Pennsylvania along Route 95. By ten thirty I am in South Carolina; suddenly I lose control of the steering wheel and go into a ditch. The car rolls over three times before it finally stops, upside down, totally demolished. Fortunately, I land in an embankment of bushes instead of crashing into a tree or overpass. I find myself hanging upside down, with my windshield completely smashed. People stop their cars and help me exit the mashed-up mess that was once my car.

As we walk up the embankment to Route 95, about forty yards from where I crashed, the police ask us, "Who was driving that car?" I answer, "Me." A fireman brought to the scene says, "God bless you. That car is completely totaled and you don't have a scratch. Do you know that you're lucky to be alive? And are you sure you're all right?" I answer, "Yes, why?" He tells me that rapid speech is usually an indication that a person is in trauma. I respond, "Oh, I talk fast all the time."

It takes two tow trucks to get my car out, since it is so far down in the ditch that the first truck gets stuck. They drive me to an auto repair shop and then to the nearest airport, where I rent a car and continue on my merry way to Pennsylvania. I stay overnight in a hotel somewhere in Virginia and then make my way to the board meeting right on time. My fellow board members cannot get over what happened and my determination to make the meeting. On Monday morning I drop off the rental car in Manhattan on my way to work.

A Rohs Family Dark Side

One Saturday afternoon in 1986 I drive with my cousin Andy to Apollo Street in Greenpoint, Brooklyn. I am on pins and needles because Andy has convinced me to take the next step and meet the children of my father's first wife, Linda, and their kids. I have no desire to meet them but Andy thinks it is a good idea. Besides, it's at a block party, which I'd never attended, and I'm curious to see what that's about.

When we arrive on Apollo Street I am all eyes and ears. It is a working-class community made up entirely of attached row or town houses. I am paranoid as can be and hope that I don't stick out like a tomato. Music is blasting; kids and adolescents are playing in the street. Everything seems to be going along fine until I see one of the neighborhood teenagers. His face is smeared with black shoe polish so that he looks like a caricature of a black man. Folks are laughing. I had heard about things like that, and it is grotesque.

I tell Andy I want to leave. He is also embarrassed because he is trying to link me up with my family, but with the kid in blackface and everyone thinking it's a joke, well, it is not going the way my cousin planned. But he's still hoping.

So he introduces me to my half brother, who introduces me to his son. We speak briefly. I learn that my nephew is a detective at a precinct on Empire Boulevard in Brooklyn. He in turn introduces me to his son—my half brother's grandson—who is an eight-year-old blond-haired boy. To make small talk, I ask the kid if he plays basketball because I figure every eight-year-old plays basketball. His response is, "No way! That's a nigger sport." I am completely flabbergasted and at a loss for words, but I chide him.

"That's not a nice thing to say about people."

His father, the detective, hears me correcting his son and tells me with some pride in his voice, "He got that from me." He is proud of himself!

Andy now knows it is all over, but before I make my escape I take the time to ask my nephew how can he talk like that when he works in a multicultural community. He says, "I smile to their faces but I'm transferring to Staten Island where folks know how to put them in their place." Yuck!

I ask Cousin Andy to get me out of there. And after this incident I never have any interest in meeting any other family members.

13   **Reflections**

No child should grow up in an institution. My upbringing was harsh, with little in the way of pleasurable ease, not much nurturing, and many unanswered questions and unacknowledged needs. By and large, I was raised by people who made do with little. The Sisters of Mercy and Marianist Brothers worked long hours in a system that stretched them beyond the limits. Only the strength of their calling kept most of them from breaking. It is with some relief that I can say that today society understands there is no perfect, one-size-fits-all "answer" to the question of care for vulnerable children.

In 1964, the year before I left St. Vincent's Home, President Lyndon Johnson initiated the Great Society agenda, generally known as the War on Poverty, under which federal entitlements were funded for adults and children who, for one reason or another, were not prospering in U.S. society. Billions were sent to the states to enhance educational, health, and human services. In the foster care world, opportunities I could have only dreamed of became available, serendipitously coinciding with innovations in child welfare theories and practices.

For example, at St. Vincent's, several initiatives were launched:

1. Foster boarding homes were created, where children of all ages would be placed with a suitable family rather than in congregate care (often in large, campus settings).
2. Group foster homes were instituted, where teenagers would live in a large one-family house in a regular neighborhood, supervised

by specialized agency staff, often a married couple, who would care for and raise eight to twelve adolescents.

3. A physical and programmatic renovation of its large residence (St. Vincent's Home) for 150 boys was undertaken. Dormitories were converted into rooms and recreation space and programs were expanded. Food services were enhanced to be tasty and enjoyable as well as nutritional, and available whenever a child felt hungry.

4. Professional teams were designed for each child. Childcare workers, social workers, and clinicians combined their collective talents to guide and ensure the child's growth and development. Natural families, whenever possible, were engaged to support and inspire. Whenever advisable, the team prepared the child to live with his or her family and then discharged the child to the family's care.

5. Educational reinforcement entered into every child's life, wherever and whenever needed—in the foster boarding homes, in the group homes and at the main residence. Children who were ready and who expressed the desire often went to private and Catholic schools. A college program was initiated, and even today St. Vincent's boasts of its numerous college graduates. The agency's objective became "No more welfare; instead, thriving careers."

6. Family involvement was initiated and enhanced so that the children were in touch with their roots and developed loving relationships with their relatives, which encouraged them to quickly and steadily become children of worth.

As the childcare field developed in the 1980s and 1990s, very large residences and institutions were nicknamed "warehouses," sometimes unfairly, depending on a child's experience. As foster boarding homes expanded and community-based group homes multiplied, each with more and more specialized services for distinct populations, the large residences/institutions gave way.

Simultaneously, more options became available, particularly subsidized adoptions and kinship foster care. Foster families who were
willing and fit to adopt foster children but lacked sufficient independent income to do so were subsidized by the state. More recently,
government has turned its attention to adoptions that were shaky or
failed because those children still require services. Like any human
endeavor, there is success and failure!

Allowing relatives to become foster parents moved many, many
children from congregate and boarding home care to live with loving
relatives under an agency's supervision. This opportunity is particularly advantageous for large sibling groups of children, preadoles-
cents, and adolescents.

As foster care entered the twenty-first century, government began preventive programs. When a family is at risk of having their
children enter foster care because of "family troubles," social workers
are sent to the family home to intervene and restore family functioning, so that the children remain within their family. Overall, it has
been successful, but government budget challenges limit the number
of families that can be helped in this manner.

Another dimension of more recent child welfare practice is
neighborhood development, also called Promise Neighborhoods,
Community Development Programs, and the like. The purpose is to
have human services immediately available with adequate resources
in the neighborhood to assist families at risk. The more immediate
localized services, the less trauma and stress around the problem.
St. Vincent's Services has been set up to address all these issues.

St. Vincent's Mental Health Services, which began in 1967 just
for its own foster children, now serves several communities (adults
and children) while treating foster children from several foster care
agencies. Good mental health, like physical health, is the point where
services need to begin and be maintained. Often, mental health, or
what is increasingly being called behavioral health, is the core service, with the social and educational services wrapped around it according to personality and primary health needs. Today, even when

the problem is called "educational," "social," or "economic," there is hardly a situation without a mental health component to it.

Over the years, I have been asked what was good and bad about my experience in institutions, and which practices and policies helped or hindered me.

On the good side, first and foremost, I learned discipline and structure through consistency. I always knew what to expect. The rules and regulations were very clear, as were the consequences for breaking them. I learned how to live with others in a group. And I learned how to get along with everyone, regardless of where they came from and the color of their skin. I learned the value of community—we were all Vinnie Boys. And, for the most part, other than those two serious incidents (which were committed by a layperson and an out-of-town religious visitor), I felt safe and secure during those nineteen years of care.

My involvement with people and places outside the homes helped me as well. Even though I did not realize it, having a significant person like an Aunt Katherine during my years in care connected me to the outside world. The abundance of recreational activities that were available to me, such as belonging to the Pop Warner and CYO sports organizations and going to Camp Christopher, allowed me to get outside my immediate experience and learn the values of exercise, teamwork, and commitment, while exposing me to whole worlds outside of the Catholic homes in which I lived. The civic and fraternal organizations, like the Knights of Columbus, Holy Name Society, Rotary Club, Elks Club, fire department, and police department, lifted all our spirits, despite our personal circumstances. Having a social worker or other professional search for biological family members helped lessen my sense of being alone and lost. Being an altar boy and performing at the Brooklyn Academy of Music as a member of the tap dancing team (not to mention the other teams I played on) taught me to always be competitive and to give 100 percent to everything I did.

On the negative side, some practices were downright bad and have had lasting impact. The practice of housing twenty-two to seventy-two youngsters in large open dormitories with one or two caregivers caused many of us to get lost in the system. The institutional environment—being given a simple twin bed and a locker and a chair, and, sometimes, a cubicle—did not provide any semblance of a home. I grew up with the feeling that I was just a number, not a person. There was no sense of privacy. The staff could not give us individual attention; caregivers had no choice but to concentrate solely on control and discipline. We had no opportunity for them to teach us acceptable behavior and how to relate to adults, peers, and significant others.

In the institutions where I lived we were pretty much left on our own, outside of following the rules and regulations, and we were given no recourse to deal with problems or emergencies. No IDs with name and address, no medical condition cards, no emergency phone numbers, no clinical services on-site, no child advocates, and no opportunity to speak of concerns in confidence. Few of the nonspecialized staff were trained, and there was no coordination of care or follow-up. For example, a particular psychological test I was given governed how and why I was in care. I was never reevaluated in the nearly two decades I was in care. Although they tried to prepare us for moving on to the next institution by telling us we were going (and had to go, because of our age), there was no real discharge planning.

None of the institutions in which I lived had any programs in place to prepare us for independent living upon final discharge. There was no discussion about financial matters such as opening a checking account or how to pay rent. No discussion of how to maintain health. No attention paid to how to live in an apartment, buy food and cook it, do laundry, how to become involved in your community, or what it meant to be a good citizen. I had to learn all these things on my own.

My life has been a strange journey. I am acutely aware that my happy ending was made possible in large part because of the people who

THE CITY OF NEW YORK
OFFICE OF THE MAYOR
NEW YORK, N.Y. 10007

May 4, 2006

Dear Friends:

I am pleased to send greetings to all those gathered for the 36th Annual Awards Dinner of the Fordham University Graduate School of Social Service Alumni Association.

Since the late 1800s, social workers have provided essential services to our nation's hospitals, non-profit organizations, and government agencies, and have helped Americans overcome life's challenges and society's injustices. Tonight, I am pleased to recognize the talented alumni of the Graduate School of Social Service for their many years of dedicated service and invaluable contributions to the residents of New York City.

I also join with the Association in recognizing its honorees: Edward Rohs, recipient of the Dr. Mary Ann Quaranta Award; and Susan Grady, recipient of the Ralph DeMayo Award. These two outstanding social workers have improved the quality of life of our City's most vulnerable residents, and I commend them on a lifetime of service that continues to better the lives of others. In addition, I thank Mr. Rohs and Ms. Grady for their support of Fordham University, the Graduate School of Social Service, and the Alumni Association.

Please accept my best wishes for a memorable event and for continued success.

Sincerely,

Michael R. Bloomberg
Mayor

A commendation from the mayor of New York.

cared enough to come forward when I was young. When I came of age, there were people with whom I formed the close bonds that have sustained me through the years. At the beginning of my story, I mentioned that on the night I received a prestigious award I had a breakthrough and spoke for the first time about my early years,

Congressional Record

United States of America

PROCEEDINGS AND DEBATES OF THE 109th CONGRESS, FIRST SESSION

House of Representatives

TRIBUTE TO EDWARD ROHS

HON. BILL PASCRELL, JR.

OF NEW JERSEY

Thursday, May 4, 2006

Mr. PASCRELL of New Jersey. Mr. Speaker, I would like to call to your attention the work of an outstanding individual, Edward Rohs, who was recognized on May 4, 2006 for his dedication to helping his community in the field of Social Services.

It is only fitting that Edward Rohs be honored, in this, the permanent record of the greatest freely elected body on Earth, for he has a long history of caring, leadership, creativity, and commitment to his noble profession.

Mr. Rohs began his professional career as an investigator in the Brooklyn district attorney's office. Ed soon realized however that his true passion was for helping children and families. Ed decided to return to his alma mater, Fordham University, to earn his Master's degree in Social Work Administration, working while attending classes as a child care worker, a supervisor, and a camp director at several child care agencies.

In 1982 upon completing his studies and graduating with his MSW, he began working for the Administration for Children's Services in New York City. He was asked to become a part of a team that was formed to ensure that the children in the care of the foster care agencies under contract with the city were doing their job to help the most disadvantaged of its young residents. After becoming a certified social worker, he also worked part time at a mental health clinic in Brooklyn, providing psychotherapy and counseling.

In 1987, Ed moved on to the Office of Behavioral Health at the New York City Health and Hospital Corporation. In this capacity, he monitored the psychiatric emergency care at eleven acute care hospitals. He later worked as a senior program planning analyst for the New York City Department of Health and Mental Hygiene. Since 1997, he has been employed at the New York State Office of Mental Health, and serves as the Borough Coordinator in Manhattan and Staten Island.

Since graduating, Ed has remained an important part of the Fordham community. He volunteered as a weight training coach for the Rams Men's basketball team from 1982 to 1999. Over those seventeen years, Ed not only helped the team members grow stronger athletically and academically, but also made lifelong friendships. He currently serves as president of the Fordham University Graduate School of Social Service Alumni Association.

Outside his career and service to his alma mater, Ed, a resident of Brooklyn, serves on the board of directors of the Lake Adventure Community Association, in Milford, PA. His positive influence on all those he encounters is especially evident in his large circle of friends and family, especially Sister Johanna McLoughlin, S.M., his niece Dana Floyd, and his god children.

The job of a United States Congressman involves so much that is rewarding, yet nothing compares to learning about and recognizing the efforts of individuals like Edward Rohs. As a fellow alumnus of Fordham University, I am proud to bestow this honor onto Edward Rohs.

Mr. Speaker, I ask that you join our colleagues, Ed's family and friends, all those whose lives have been influenced by Ed, and me in recognizing the outstanding and invaluable service of Mr. Edward Rohs.

Honored in *The Congressional Record.*

In Memoriam

Sister Johanna and Aunt Katherine.

My Aunt Katherine died of heart failure in 1980. When I visited her in Lutheran Medical Center shortly before her death, she made me promise that I would take care of her sister Johanna. For thirty years I tried to keep my promise and to pay back what Katherine McCarthy had given me. Every Thanksgiving, Christmas, and Easter, Johanna and I went to visit Katherine's gravesite at the National Cemetery in Farmingdale, New York. Then we would go out to dinner.

On September 3, 2010, Sister Mary Johanna McLaughlin, my dear Johanna, passed away as well.

shocking colleagues and bringing friends to tears. In fact, that night I received three awards, the first being the Dr. Mary Ann Quaranta Award for outstanding services to children and families given by the Fordham University Social Services Alumni Association, on whose board I was honored to serve for several years. On this wonderful night, I was also awarded the Dean's Leadership Award. And unexpectedly, Congressman Bill Pascrell of the 8th District of New Jersey presented me with the Congressional Record Award for outstanding services to children and families.

Sitting in the audience were members of my self-made family, dear friends and their children, people whose lives have intertwined with mine, people I chose and who have chosen me—the Perez family, the Floyd family, the Pascrells, Sister Johanna, Ramon Nieto, Alison Passy, and Fordham's former president, Fr. Joseph A. O'Hare— they were all present to toast my achievements and celebrate my life. They, along with former Vinnie Boys and players I have coached, are my family. They form the fabric of my life. I am blessed.

Postscript: September 11, 2001

Following 9/11, my office assigned me to provide assistance to the local governmental mental health agency. The 9/11 emergency health center started out at the Lexington Avenue Armory, but it was immediately inundated with people needing multiple emergency service assistance in areas that ran the gamut from social services and mental health services to emergency access to food and clothing. When it ran out of space, the agency moved to Pier 92. Compounding the tragedy was the stark reality that many of the victims had been their family's primary wage earner. People were grieving and in need of material assistance.

One day, while working on the pier, I saw a police officer snap at a person who was standing on line waiting for assistance. When I brought it to his attention, he said, "Look, I'm sorry. But I've been working twelve to sixteen hours, seeing all this sorrow and misery firsthand. All these people are getting services. But what about us police officers who are also under extreme stress and burned out? We need help also."

I was so moved that I promised the police officer I would bring his concerns to the command post in our office. I learned that other colleagues, including Dr. Michael Lesser, medical director at the New York City Department of Health and Mental Hygiene, and Assistant Commissioner Isaac Monserrate, were hearing the same story. Shortly thereafter, the New York City Police Department, Fire Department, and Emergency Medical Services all received funding to assist our first responders.

We know how people came together in the aftermath of this devastating event. Less talked about is the remarkable partnership that developed among the private, public, and nonprofit sectors. There were no turf battles and no pettiness. Besides the American Red Cross, all kinds of trade organizations came together to help. Even before the federal, state, and city funding started coming in to assist the thousands of families affected by this attack, agencies stepped up and used their limited resources. It is an event I will never forget, especially accompanying families that lost loved ones down to Ground Zero and standing in the pit, smelling all the toxic fumes.

Appendixes

Appendix A

Vinnie Boys in the World

* Vinnie Boy of St. Vincent's Home before Ed Rohs.
** Vinnie Boy of St. Vincent's Home during Ed Rohs's tenure.
*** Vinnie Boy of St. Vincent's Home after Ed Rohs.

John Babich: New York City Department of Sanitation worker (retired).**

Joseph Dowd, JD: New York State Supreme Court judge; New York State assemblyman; New York City public school teacher.*

James Dubonet, MSW: Owner of a pest control company; social worker (retired); Ed Rohs's dorm counselor at SVH.*

Al Fuentes, MSW: Car dealer; social worker (retired); Ed Rohs's dorm counselor at SVH.*

Orgie Graham: Detective, New York City Police Department.*

John London: Accountant in New York City.**

John McConnell, JD: Attorney in private practice.***

John McGinley, MS: St. Francis Prep School teacher (retired); former director of childcare at St. Vincent's Home.*

Carlos Melendez: Works in the private sector.**

James Melendez: Works in the private sector.**

Ramon Nieto, Sr.: New York State corrections officer (retired); Golden Gloves champion.***

Carlos Passy, MSW: Assistant principal in Florida (retired); social worker.**

Harry Perez: U.S. Postal Service worker (retired); diamond cutter.**

Richard River: Detective, New York City Police Department.**

Andrew Velez, MA: New York City public school teacher (retired).**

Freddy Velez: Private investigator.***

Teddy Velez: New York City Department of Sanitation worker (retired).**

Joseph Walters, MD: Cardiologist.***

Appendix B

The Foundling Hospital

In the 1800s in New York City, the government had no provision for the care of abandoned babies and very small children. Each year, thousands were abandoned to alleyways and trash heaps around the city. Those found alive on the streets were taken by the police to a prison and workhouse known as Blackwell's Island. There the infants and small children were cared for by aging prisoners. Not surprisingly, few survived infancy. Mothers also left infants at the doors of religious schools and convents.

Sr. Mary Irene Fitzgibbon of the Sisters of Charity was a novice in the order when she began to observe an increase in the number of abandoned babies being left at the doors of her convent and the school where she taught. Having emigrated from London, she knew about foundling asylums in Europe, and she had the vision to understand that New York City was in desperate need of a similar system.

With church approval, she organized a women's society that raised enough money to rent a house on West 12th Street. They took residence in October 1869 and planned to open the doors to what they called the New York Foundling Asylum on January 1, 1870. But the need was so great that by the time the doors officially opened, they already had 123 babies in residence.

The system was simple. A white cradle was placed in the foyer and the front door was unlocked. A desperate mother could enter and leave her child, with no questions asked. All she had to do was ring the bell to alert the sisters that another infant had been brought to their door. The asylum was filling a desperate need, and by the end of its first year it had outgrown its quarters.

They moved to a new, larger house at 3 Washington Square North, and shortly thereafter the New York State Assembly authorized New York City to cede the block between 68th and 69th Streets and Lexington and Third Avenues. The city was also authorized to match $100,000 to be raised by private donations for a building fund. The women's society that Sr. Mary Irene had created raised $100,000, the city matched it, and the new building opened in 1873. It not only provided care for infants and unwed mothers, but also offered adoption services for children who were legally free to be adopted. The city provided support for the daily care of children at the residence, paying forty-five cents a day for each child under two years of age, and thirty-two cents for children over two years old. Catholic charities and donors also contributed. While the building was in progress, the asylum became a refuge for unmarried mothers.

In 1880 St. Anne's Maternity Pavilion was erected, in order to shelter expectant mothers who were in need and to provide proper care for them during their confinement. It remained in operation until 1945.

By legal enactment in 1891, "The Foundling Asylum," the organization's name under which it was incorporated in 1869, was changed to "The New York Foundling Hospital."

Today, the New York Foundling Hospital provides a variety of services that expand their mission, including nursery care on an emergency basis to abandoned and neglected children; casework services to families requesting placement of children; the placement and supervision of Catholic children in boarding and adoption homes; aftercare supervision of children discharged from foster care; and shelter care and casework services to unmarried mothers.

For more on the Foundling Hospital, see Thomas Meehan, "Sister Irene," *The Catholic Encyclopedia* (New York: Robert Appleton Company, 1910), vol. 8, available at http://www.newadvent.org/cathen/08131a.htm and http://www.orphantraindepot.com/NYFH History.html.

Appendix C

Suggested Reading

Bogen, Hyman. *The Luckiest Orphans: A History of the Hebrew Orphan Asylum of New York.* Champaign: University of Illinois Press, 1992.

Cmiel, Kenneth. *A Home of Another Kind.* Chicago: University of Chicago Press, 1995.

Crenson, Matthew. *Building the Invisible Orphanage.* Cambridge, Mass.: Harvard University Press, 1998.

Freedman, Renna S. *These Are Our Children: Jewish Orphanages in the United States, 1880–1925.* Hanover, N.H.: University Press of New England, 1994.

Hacsi, Timothy A. *Second Home: Orphan Asylums and Poor Families in America.* Cambridge, Mass.: Harvard University Press, 1997.

Hadler, Susan J., and Ann B. Mix. *Lost in the Victory: Reflections of American War Orphans of World War II.* Denton: University of North Texas Press, 1998.

McKenzie, Richard B. *The Home: A Memoir of Growing up in an Orphanage.* New York: Basic Books, 1996.

Patterson, James J. *America's Struggle Against Poverty in the Twentieth Century.* Cambridge, Mass.: Harvard University Press, 2000.

Seraile, William. *Angels of Mercy: White Women and the History of New York's Colored Orphan Asylum.* New York: Fordham University Press, 2011.

Shaw, Richard. *Dagger John: The Unquiet Life and Times of Archbishop John Hughes of New York.* New York: Paulist Press, 1977.

Wagner, David. *The Poorhouse: America's Forgotten Institution.* Lanham, Md.: Rowman & Littlefield, 2005.

Notes

1. The Search for Solutions

"the poorhouse," "the poor farm," or "the workhouse": In England it was called "the almshouse."

"attend to orphans and minor children within the jurisdiction of this city": Adriana E. van Zwieten, "The Orphan Chamber of New Amsterdam," *William and Mary Quarterly,* 3rd ser., 53, no. 2 (April 1996): 319–40.

source of revenue for government: David Wagner, *The Poorhouse: America's Forgotten Institution* (Lanham, Md.: Rowman & Littlefield, 2005).

its sister city across the water, Brooklyn: Brooklyn was an independent city until its consolidation with New York City in 1898.

2. New York City in the Nineteenth Century

malaria, yellow fever, and cholera: See xroads.virginia.edu/~HYPER/DETOC/transport/workers.html.

"no shoes and no hat": James Dabney McCabe, *Lights and Shadows of New York* (Philadelphia: National Publishing Company, 1872), 739.

"they wanted it at fifty cents": "Newsboys Strike," *New York Times,* October 14, 1884, http://query.nytimes.com/mem/archive-free/pdf?res=9A0 7E7D6163AEF33A25757C1A9669D94659FD7CF.

"remain in the Asylum": George Paul Jacoby, *Catholic Childcare in New York* (Washington, D.C.: Catholic University of America Press, 1941), 115.

"any unlawful game to play": Ibid., 118.

boutique shop selling luxury merchandise: Ibid., 117.

"pouring water on them": See http://www.digitalhistory.uh.edu/database/article_display.cfm?HHID=166.

other states followed: Indiana, Illinois, Iowa, Kansas, Kentucky, Missouri, North and South Dakota, and Ohio.

"meet them at the hotel at the time above": See http//www.orphan traindepot.com/OrphanTrainAnnouncement.htm/.

3. The Twentieth Century

the tenor of these family reunions: Susan Johnson Hadler and Ann Bennett Mix, *Lost in the Victory* (Chapel Hill: University of North Carolina Press, 1982).

brought to the doors of the Foundling Hospital: In 1998, the U.S. Department of Health and Human Services received 105 reports of babies abandoned in public places across the country—approximately one-twelfth the number reported in New York alone 130 years before.

4. The Sisters of Mercy: A Tale of Two Cities

"expose them in a foreign land": John R. G. Hassard, *Life of the Most Reverend John Hughes, D.D.* (New York: D. Appleton and Company, 1866), 309.

did not have a doctor aboard: For more information about sailing vessels from Ireland to North America, see http://www.finnvalley.ie/history/emigration/index.html.

they also provided religious instruction: Sr. Mary Josephine Gately, *Historical Sketches, 1831–1931* (New York: Macmillan, 1931).

Brooklyn Eagle: Back issues of the *Brooklyn Eagle* are available at the Brooklyn Public Library.

immigrants who lived in misery: In 2000, according to U.S. Census data, 28 percent were foreign-born (931,000).

5. My Earliest Years

1950s to teach kindergarten: David Gonzalez, "After 146 Years, a Brooklyn Convent Is Closing," *New York Times,* December 16, 2008, http://www.nytimes.com/2008/12/17/nyregion/17convent.html.

8. St. Vincent's Home for Boys

alleviate the suffering of indigent newsboys: John K. Sharp, *History of the Diocese of Brooklyn, 1857–1953: The Catholic Church on Long Island* (New York: Fordham University Press, 1954), 1:205.

"without benefit of education or religion": *Golden Jubilee,* 1905.

"earn an honest and honorable livelihood": Saint Vincent's Home for Boys, official journal in commemoration of the Diamond Jubilee, 1944, 17–23.

"twenty pounds of beef": *Brooklyn Eagle,* December 28, 1880.

"more useful than newsboys and bootblacks": Thomas de Cantillon Church, "Father Drumgoole's Work," *Donahoe's Magazine,* September 1879, 199.

the social workers took turns: For fifty-six years, St. Vincent's Home, now St. Vincent's Services, has continued to conduct this annual fundraiser. Although the St. George Hotel and Camp Christopher no longer exist, an annual dinner is now held the Monday before Thanksgiving at the Waldorf Astoria in Manhattan and supports the American Dream Program for former St. Vincent's residents who want to attend college.

11. Inventing Another New Life

home of the popular adventure novelist: Other Zane Grey museums were located in Norwich, Ohio, and in Payson, Arizona.

12. Milestones

Steven Samuels and James Robinson: In addition to Steve Samuels and James Robinson, over the seventeen years of volunteering I provided individual guidance and mentoring to other student-athletes, among them Fred Herzog, Connie Mack, and others.

Fordham basketball great Bevon Robin: Robin was the third-highest scorer in Fordham history.

PA, SSI: PA means public assistance for people who have reached the national poverty threshold; SSI means Social Security income provided to people with a mental illness that prevents them from holding down a job.

Index